The Wonders of You

The Wonders

UNDERSTANDING YOUR UNIQUE ENERGY

of You

Nathaniel John Goetz

O'LEARY
PUBLISHING
The Influencer's Press

NAPLES, FL

Published in the United States by

O'Leary Publishing

www.olearypublishing.com

The views, information, or opinions expressed in this book are solely those of the authors involved and do not necessarily represent those of O'Leary Publishing, LLC.

The author has made every effort possible to ensure the accuracy of the information presented in this book. However, the information herein is sold without warranty, either expressed or implied. Neither the author, publisher nor any dealer or distributor of this book will be held liable for any damages caused either directly or indirectly by the instructions or information contained in this book. You are encouraged to seek professional advice before taking any action mentioned herein.

For information on getting permission for reprints and excerpts, contact O'Leary Publishing at admin@olearypublishing.com.

ISBN: 978-1-952491-35-1 (paperback)

ISBN: 978-1-952491-34-4 (hardcover)

ISBN: 978-1-952491-36-8 (ebook)

Library of Congress Control Number: 2022900985

Printed in the United States of America

This book is dedicated to God,
from whom every good and perfect gift comes.

Contents

Preface

Do you ever feel misunderstood? Do you ever feel like you aren't connecting with others properly? Do you feel like when you speak, others seem to hear something other than what you've just said? PeopleLogics is a tool to help you overcome your frustrations – a tool that will teach you a way to not only help you understand who you are, but also how you were made. It will then be easier to understand why you get the reactions you do, as well as to understand the people with whom you are interacting.

The Wonders of You is PeopleLogics 101 – an insightful book focusing on improving human relations. PeopleLogics answers the million-dollar questions for which we rarely have answers. These are answers to questions that most of us were not taught as children or young adults: why people behave the way they do, and why they most likely will behave similarly in the future.

The primary mission of PeopleLogics is to bring unity through understanding.

No matter how much technology advances, or how much the world changes, there is one component that will never become obsolete: people. By taking the time to understand who you are, you will be better able to understand others and live a more harmonious life. With understanding comes higher self-esteem, and all the benefits that come with that development.

PeopleLogics works to impart wisdom and understanding of how to improve human relations. The topic of human relations can be – and has been – overcomplicated by many. The goal is that individuals will gain an understanding about other people that they can readily use in their everyday lives. The world is filled with too much conflict that is a result of people not understanding one another and how they are made. This misunderstanding of one's self, as well as others, causes defensiveness, which leads to unnecessary conflict. With understanding comes harmony – not only with one's self, but also with the numerous relationships we each enjoy.

When applied, PeopleLogics liberates people to be all they were created to be. It teaches people to look inside themselves first – and then they can begin to understand others. PeopleLogics teaches that it is OK to just "be yourself." It enlightens people so they can turn frustration and anger into compassion and understanding.

PeopleLogics focuses strongly on helping you understand who you are, and who you are not. After reading this book, as well as the other PeopleLogics training materials, you will have a whole new understanding of how you were made, and why people around you behave the way they do when you interact with them. You will be empowered to resolve problems and difficulties in relationships like never before.

The contents of this book will empower you with insights and an understanding about people, and your relationships. It will also help you navigate and identify the types of people you will want to surround yourself with, so you can experience your highest potential and enjoy the fullness of life that God designed for you.

If you want more love, joy and peace in your life, PeopleLogics is for you. This book was written to share the principles that my father – the founder of PeopleLogics, John Goetz – and I put together over years of research around the world. We traveled to many countries and experienced many cultures – and we found that the core principles in this book work anywhere in the world.

My prayer is that a line or an idea in this book will spark a bit of curiosity and desire in you to grow and improve relationships in your walk through life. This is not just another pop-psychology book. This book was written to help change the hearts and souls of its readers. Please lean in, enjoy, learn and grow personally from these writings. The content of this book will help make it much easier for you to find your place in the world – the place where you fit and can use your God-given gifts and talents to benefit yourself and the people around you.

Too many times, we try to understand why we cannot do the things that other people can do naturally. Consequently, we feel bad about ourselves or try to fit ourselves into situations which don't naturally suit us. PeopleLogics helps us understand who we are, and why it is beneficial to celebrate our differences. Then it becomes natural to work together to accomplish common goals and objectives.

We each have our own gifts and talents. Those gifts and talents help us enjoy life, achieve more, and make an impact in the world. It all starts with noticing and accepting the energy with which we were made.

We will never be fully successful or fulfilled doing those things that we were not naturally equipped to accomplish. Therefore, PeopleLogics can help you discover your strengths and provide access to new knowledge about yourself. Such discoveries will empower you to reach new heights of success in the many types of relationships in your life. PeopleLogics will help you focus on spending time, holding positions, and working with people who complement one another – in places that allow you to maximize your talents.

PeopleLogics helps people live a fulfilling life. When applied – it will work for you in almost any area of your life. Building a fulfilling life can be as easy as applying the principles outlined in this book. Ready? Let's dive in!

Nathaniel John Goetz

John T. Goetz
Philosopher and Successful Business Man
1941-2002

INTRODUCTION

PeopleLogics 101

The Beginnings of PeopleLogics

"It is time for the whole world to move up. I am not really interested in changing one city. I am interested in a philosophy going to the whole world to change the whole world."

JOHN T. GOETZ

Born at home, my father, John Goetz, was brought up in some of the most humble circumstances of his time. He was raised on a farm his family rented in southeast Missouri, in the Midwestern part of the United States. As soon as he was able, he was in the fields, working alongside his six brothers and sisters.

He was not able to receive much from traditional education, since he was required to stay home from school to work on the farm many weeks out of the school year. However, that did not stop him from learning. John paid close attention to life and became interested in what the people who lived near him were doing.

One event that had a major impact on John's life was standing at the bedside of his grandfather as he passed away. His grandfather was alert – using no medication to ease his pain. John told the story many times of how his grandfather would talk to people who had passed away years earlier as he was crossing over. John remembered that his grandfather said things like, "Tom, I always wondered if you made it," and, "Jim, I didn't think you would make it."

Witnessing his grandfather talking to people on the other side made a lasting impression on John. From that time on, he became keenly aware that there was more than just living here in this life. He became interested in learning about God and how to live on Earth in a way that would have eternal significance. He realized that, at best, this life was short and that he should focus on learning and doing things that would have lasting effects.

Once he left the farm, one of my father's first jobs was working in a shoe factory. That gave him the opportunity to observe different types of people; and he was amazed how many seemed to be happy working in a highly-structured environment. He knew there was something else that he was supposed to do with his life.

John had 22 jobs in 24 months. He was searching for his place in life. He was laid off from many jobs, not only because the economy was bad in his part of the country, but also because his various bosses pushed him to do work that did not fit his energy and working style. Sometimes, when his bosses would try to threaten him with a layoff, John would ask, "Can you move me to the top of that layoff list?"

Finally, John had the opportunity to move to Indiana, where he had been told he could find better work. John was a hard worker; yet, he did not feel that he was making the most of his life or using his God-given talents.

While in Indiana, he joined the National Guard to serve his country. Once again, he realized quickly that the highly-structured environment of the armed forces would not be a good fit for him to enjoy a long-term career.

John's path was full of many twists and turns. He held many more jobs and acquired a variety of skills along the way. He had been a mechanic in the National Guard, so when he returned to civilian life, he started working in an auto shop. There, he rebuilt starters and generators. Even though it was hard work, he enjoyed the creativity and challenge of getting one of those starters to work again.

He later learned how to be a brick mason, where he loved the challenge of competing with others to lay the most bricks in a day. Through it all, his connection to God remained constant.

It wasn't long before John followed what he felt was a call to become a minister. He had always found great hope and assuredness in his own faith and wanted to help people become more aware of the importance of following a love-based lifestyle that would have eternal rewards.

As an evangelist, John's lifestyle was not full of wealth or lavish earthly rewards. In fact, we lived in a travel trailer that we pulled behind our car from place to place to minister to people in small churches. There were a few years that our family was on the road 40 to 50 weeks out of the year.

During that time, John heard God say to him, "Son, I am going to take you off the road and I am going to bless you." As it turned out, in one of the last places where John was helping a small group transition from meeting in a home to a building, he was introduced to a couple. They were involved in an emerging company that sold products to help people with the health of their bodies.

John saw that working with this company would create additional income for his family and also provide him with the freedom to continue to help people improve the health of their souls. It was not long after that when John started his own business with this company and became successful in a short period of time.

John loved to talk with people – and most of all, he really loved to help people. He discovered that the best way for him to help the most people was to motivate others to build businesses with him. His charisma and high spirit were exactly the qualities that he needed to be successful. He used some of his profits to invest in real estate – and was thrilled to be able to use all of his experiences working with many types of people to gain new insights into human nature and behavior.

CHAPTER 1

How Energy Flows

Have you ever been attracted to – or repelled by – someone for seemingly no good reason? Have you ever felt misunderstood when you were communicating your feelings with, or responding to, someone with whom you were in a relationship? Have you ever wondered why it is that, even though you were the same gender as someone, there seemed to be so much difference in your behaviors?

The chapters in this book will bring understanding to you about those questions and so much more. The journey we are about to go on will not only be enjoyable, but also enlightening as well.

To start with, you are surrounded by energy, and that energy is manifesting itself in many forms. God made it the way He did for His, and our, good pleasure. What is most important to know is that energy is not static.

It moves through creation in up-and-down and linear flows, to create a balance of nature.

Since this book is about understanding your own unique energy, let us start with humans.

In humanity, we call people with energy that flows in an up-and-down manner Starters. Linear energy people, we call Finishers. The wisdom that you will be exposed to in this book is built on this fundamental principle. This simple explanation of energy will become a game-changer in your life, as we build on this principle throughout the following chapters. The concept is something you can use to improve your life – for the rest of your life. What you will learn about this principle will help you enjoy more harmony in your relationships, and will help you find more success in your career.

Much of what we will be discussing in this book is less obvious than gender differences. In the beginning, God not only made men and women, but He also made them with up-and-down and linear energies. We were formed this way by Divine design so that there would be a balance of nature on the earth.

The following chart illustrates how Starters' energy flows in a distinct up-and-down manner, spiking and falling quickly throughout their day.

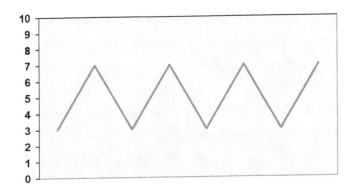

People who are made with energy that flows in a linear manner are Finishers. They are more consistent as they go through their lives. I will be elaborating on that idea in more depth in the following chapters.

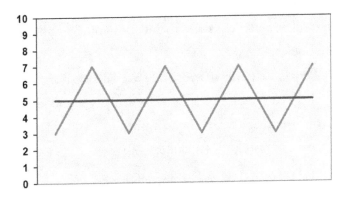

It really does not matter if you are a woman or a man. The fact is that globally, approximately half of all women are Starters and half of them are Finishers. The same is true of men – approximately half of all men are Starters and half of them are Finishers. So, there are approximately the same number of Starters and Finishers on the earth.

When you were made, you were made with, and by, energy. Many say that there are more variables to understanding human behavior. What I say is: there are over seven billion people on the planet, so a person can make this topic as complicated as they wish. The reality is that when it is all said and done, no one can change the fact that there are – and always will be – approximately an equal number of Starters and Finishers on earth.

In the process of our work, we developed some assessments that can help you discover your own energy type, and the energy type of others. With that knowledge, you will be better equipped to understand the insights in this book.

The first assessment consists of over 50 questions that can help you determine your own energy type and know if you are either a Starter or a Finisher.

Some of the choices include:

☐ I tend to talk to hear myself think.
☐ I tend to think before I speak.

☐ I prefer talking to people a lot.
☐ I prefer listening to people tell stories.

☐ I like to tell fun stories at the table.

☐ I am comfortable with some silence, and listening to others, at the table.

☐ I enjoy a short power nap in the afternoon.

☐ I find it is hard for me to take a 15-minute nap and feel refreshed.

☐ I usually arrive a few minutes late to events.

☐ I usually arrive early to an event to get a good seat.

The entire assessment can be accessed online by going to: *www.PeopleLogics.com*.

PeopleLogics training sessions – either virtual or in person – will allow you to benefit from another level of insight regarding yourself and others.

In the next two chapters, you will learn some of the characteristics of Starters and Finishers. Knowing about those characteristics will make it easier to understand and more effectively communicate with each type. You will start to become more cognizant of the people around you, and you will start to live more harmoniously with others on a daily basis even before you finish this book.

CHAPTER 2

Starters

One of the first things you will want to embrace is the fact that neither Starters nor Finishers are better than the other. What is important to understand is that each is unique and wonderfully made. Knowing how your energy flows will help you love and accept yourself, and others. It will also help you choose relationships, jobs and environments that are right for your energy type. Now let us begin with the Starters.

Starters, in particular, like to get to know people on a more personal level. Starters jump into things and can build rapport with others quickly.

The following are examples of instinctive traits and characteristics that tend to apply to Starters:

- They are spontaneous, quick-acting types of people.

- They talk to hear themselves think.

- They prefer talking to a lot of different people in social situations.

- They love to tell fun stories to help make conversations more interesting.

- They are good at enjoying short power naps during the day.

- They often arrive a few minutes late to events.

- When they get angry, they tend to get over it quickly.

- They tend to be great huggers and like a lot of physical touch.

- They make friends easily.

- They like quieter, softer music, so they do not get internally overstimulated, rather than loud music with a great beat.

- Relationships, both business and personal, are important to them – much more important than time management and efficiency.

- They can be extremely transparent and like for people to know them as a person, and what they are all about, early on in a relationship.

- They start things well, but have trouble finishing them without support from others.

- They are "all-in" kinds of people. You tend to get all of them, or none of them.

- They prefer colorful, trendy, clothing.

- They prefer face-to-face conversations.

- When they are hungry, they want to eat right away; they do not want to wait for an hour to get into a more prestegious dining establishment.

- They prefer short spontaneous trips over saving their vacation time for one big annual trip.

- They like to change the layout of the furniture in their home regularly.

- They get overwhelmed when there are too many details involved in a project.

- When they make to-do lists, they do not get stressed out if they do not finish their list right away.

- They prefer a restaurant where they can sit and talk with guests.

- They get distracted easily.

- They find it easy to let go of the past and move on, in order to maintain a good, long-term friendship.

- They enjoy spontaneously spending money more than they should.

- It seems to be fine with them to let others create the energy at events, so they can ride in on it and enjoy it.

- They have a problem keeping up with their keys and sunglasses.

- When they eat, they want to eat with people, instead of eating quickly on their own.

- When it comes to food, they live to eat rather than eat to live.

- They are naturally good at casting a vision that people can embrace and help to complete.

- Customarily, they are driven by their emotions more than logic.

- They prefer many small gifts during the holidays, instead of one or two large gifts of the same value.

- They prefer to base decisions and activities on their feelings, instead of analyzing all the facts.

- They like to try new and exciting things.

- They are the ones who speak up when there is silence in a conversation.

- They prefer working with a team of people instead of working alone on a project.

- They are OK with only understanding the general concept of something.

- They prefer to have a large, immediate family. Globally, Starter women choose to have the most children.

- They prefer to tell compelling stories – and they like to start from the beginning.

- Innately, they are feelings-oriented people.

- They are very social people.

- They are some of the most expressive people on the planet.

- When they talk, they like to use their hands to express themselves.

- They prefer to make up quickly with their partner when there is a disagreement.

- They have little problem showing their feelings.

- Globally, they tend to be flexible people.

- Other than with a verbal punishment, they find it hard to discipline people – especially their children.

- They find it hard to say "no" and stick with their position.

- It is important that they are given a safe space to think out loud around others when working on a project, or when communicating with family and friends.

- They get overstimulated when there are too many televisions and/or loud music in their environment.

- They do not like to work on repetitive projects, in the same work environment, for a long period of time.

- They like to hurry and get their jobs done quickly.

- They do not mind talking about subjects that some would consider small talk – not going too deep as they are getting to know someone.

- Globally, Starters are particularly good at asking questions and getting to know a person before getting down to business with them.

- When they meet new people, curious Starters might find the person's backstory so intriguing that it could delay the actual purpose of the meeting.

- They are good at getting a person to let down their guard, no matter how defensive they might be. That can allow the person to get more comfortable with the Starter so they can develop a deeper relationship.

As you can see, Starters are amazing people and an amazing gift to the planet.

Now that we have a basic understanding of who Starters are, let us take a look into the nature of the Finishers.

CHAPTER 3

Finishers

In the last chapter, you learned that Starters are highly relational. In this chapter, you will learn that Finishers are the more task-oriented and analytical people on the planet.

Finishers are good at embracing the essence of the content being discussed, which allows them to focus on the necessary details that must be addressed to accomplish the vision.

When Finishers are given challenging jobs, they feel like people have more confidence in their ability to produce great results.

The following are examples of instinctive traits and characteristics that tend to apply to Finishers:

- They think longer before they speak. They are usually more calculating and direct with their words.

- Given the opportunity, they prefer listening to people tell stories instead of telling the stories themselves.

- They like to arrive early to events to get a good seat.

- They prefer to keep the details of their lives more private.

- They like to master the tasks that they do each and every day in order to become more efficient in their work.

- They like to take their time when working on a project in order to get each thing done correctly.

- They like the stability that comes with mastering a challenging job.

- They get to the point quickly when they speak.

- Globally, Finishers tend to prefer more formal relationships with people.

- They find it easy to stay focused.

- They prefer classic, conservative clothing.

- They are more comfortable with silence, and with listening to others, at the dinner or conference table.

- When they get angry, it takes them a while to process their emotions and the situation that needs to be resolved.

- When hungry, they tend to choose to wait for a good meal at a fine restaurant, rather than eating right away somewhere else.

- They like to save money so they can buy high-quality things.

- They are fact-oriented people. They want to know most of the facts first, before deciding to work on a project.

- They like to take their time and research multiple options before making decisions.

- They like to save up money for emergencies that may occur.

- Given the choice, Finishers would prefer to receive one or two larger gifts during the holidays, instead of many small gifts.

- They are more structured.

- They like to process their thoughts internally before they speak and share their ideas and conclusions.

- Globally, they tend to be deep thinkers.

- They take their time to plan events.

- They are the ones that are better at eating to live instead of living to eat.

- Finishers are more deliberate with their words when they are communicating.

- They like to take their time to think things through before they get excited about new ideas.

- They prefer to discipline people up front when they see a mistake, instead of dealing with the consequences of a mistake at a later time.

- They are usually more reserved socially.

- They usually like to sit, think and ponder on what is being said.

- They do not mind working by themselves to see that things get done properly.

- If they are five or ten minutes late to an appointment, they feel like they have failed themselves and their standards.

- Relationships generally have more of a purpose than a meaning.

- They make most decisions based on facts, and not so much on emotions.

- Many times they find themselves choosing to, or having to, complete projects that other people have started.

- They like to find the best layout for their furniture and keep it that way for a while.

- They prefer email or text messages in order to communicate quickly.

- They usually have a system that they use so that they always know where their keys and sunglasses are kept.

- They want to know the rules before they get started.

- Once they put something on their list, they will do their best to see that it gets finished, no matter how long it takes.

- They are more reserved when it comes to sharing their ideas.

- They prefer to have a well-thought-out purpose for the things they say and do.

- They want to know as many details as possible, in order to understand what they are being asked to accomplish.

- They tend to be very efficient while shopping. When they go to the store, they like to take a list, check the items off, and then leave as quickly as possible.

- They prefer to hide their feelings and emotions from others, bottling them up to be released at a later date.

- They prefer to get to the point in a conversation so they can get on to the next subject or project.

- When they talk, as long as they can hear the other person, they are less likely to think that they need to see the facial expressions of others to understand what they are saying.

- They generally prefer to have a smaller family, so they have the option of devoting more time to a successful career.

- If they have an argument within a personal relationship, it usually takes extra time to process their feelings.

- Generally, they prefer side hugs and patting when they hug openly.

- They are emotionally strong people who enjoy being in control of outcomes.

- They think through their position, and are firm about sticking with their decisions.

- It does not bother them to meet people in a restaurant and eat with multiple televisions and loud music playing.

To wrap it up, Finishers are people you want to have on your team, and by your side.

Both Starters and Finishers are uniquely gifted, and add value to life. By understanding their unique energy types, they can appreciate each other's differences and make accommodations for one another's strengths and weaknesses. This up-and-down, or linear, energy is not something that can be changed. Once you embrace the way you are made, and work with others based on how they are made, life can become much more enjoyable.

In the next chapter, we will be discussing how to balance the strengths of each energy type with the other so we can best use the traits imparted to each of us by our Creator. The goal is to enjoy harmonious relationships with others. Keeping the energy scales balanced is what is necessary to achieve peace on earth, and harmony within our own personal relationships.

CHAPTER 4

Balancing the Scales

By Divine design, the energies of Starters and Finishers are much different. They are different in order to balance the scales of nature, and create the most productive and cohesive environment possible. Both Starters and Finishers are a part of God's imparted design; they contrast and complement each other. When embraced, the knowledge of Starters' and Finishers' predictable behaviors will help us understand those with whom we are interacting, as well as who will be the best fit for us as partners – personally and professionally.

Starters value relationships so much that they are usually the ones who say to others, "If they will fit around the table, let them come."

One way you can tell a Starter is by their ability to touch physically in a very caring, connecting way. They are also the ones who give the best and longest hugs.

Finishers usually are more comfortable with formal relationships, which shows when someone tries to pull them in for a soft, big, warm hug.

During the COVID pandemic, people were told to social-distance from each other. At the end of a watch party that I attended, the lady of the house said to people as they were leaving, "Come on over and give me a hug. At least if I die, I will die hugging." She was a Starter.

Starters need to get on projects and get them over quickly, so that their energy, enthusiasm and attention are not lost in the process. They are "all-in" people. Most of the time, you either have 100 percent of them or you have almost nothing.

On the other hand, Finishers like to take their time, and methodically go at a desirable pace that does not get them overly stressed. That way, they can pace themselves to meet deadlines. They will also keep working over the long term to see that things are administered and running efficiently.

Starters can usually envision the best concepts and ideas. Many times, ideas come from Starters who are simply sharing their thoughts about a topic in conversation. They may not even know that they have voiced an idea. But a Finisher involved in the conversation may already have latched onto it and started to think about how to implement it. Starters tend to start talking about their ideas without considering that Finishers are prone to think about implementation even before the idea has been thoroughly discussed.

For example, a lady told me about how she used to go shopping for clothes. She would try on clothes at different stores, searching for something she wanted to take home and wear. After a couple hours of going from store to store, she would be ready to leave the shopping center. Her husband would ask her if she bought anything. She would say "No, I did not," and that she was ready to go get something to eat. Her husband would scratch his head and ask, "Are you telling me that you did all of that shopping, and you are not going to buy a thing?" He could not understand how she could leave all these stores and feel satisfied when she had bought nothing to take home with her to wear. But she would say that she did feel satisfied, because she was only trying on her feelings.

That is the way with Starters. They may not know exactly if what they are saying is correct when they are processing their thoughts. They may only be trying on the feeling of whether a thought or idea fits into their lives at a particular moment. *Would this be a good thing that we might want to do this week, or sometime in the future?*

They are thinking out loud and processing their feelings in front of their audience to see what fits the best. Finishers tend to think things through internally longer, since, to them, words tend to carry a much heavier weight.

Hearing all of the chatter, a Finisher may think that the Starter wants ideas acted upon right away. The Starter knows that something may need to be done about an idea; however, they do not necessarily think that the idea needs to be implemented right away. Often, Starters just think out loud about a topic, to hear what their spirit is saying through them for the first time. Starters usually have so many things going on in their heads that they need a safe place to think out loud and discuss possible plans of action – or, to consider whether their ideas are good enough in the first place.

One of my Starter friends has learned how to handle this kind of situation very well. He has learned to preface his statements with, "It's just an idea. I am just thinking out loud." So, when he's thinking out loud, it does not mean he wants to take action right away. His concept may not be a good idea at all. He would like to simply talk about the idea to see if anything comes of it.

Generally, Finishers love task or action item lists that accumulate over time. Once something or someone gets on their list, it is hard to get it or them off – even though it seems as if nothing is getting done to check off the items. Finishers usually are not content until the entire list is done and checked off, even if it takes years.

For example, writing this book has been on my own list for years. Many people have evaporated from my life over those years; they probably believed that the book would never be completed. As an enlightened Finisher, I have always kept it on my list as something that I need to complete in order to be obedient to God – to do what I was told to do.

Just because there was not a book to put into people's hands does not mean it was not still inside of me. Even though I have been distracted and gone off course hundreds of times over the years, I was still developing and refining the book's message. I wanted the book to contain the truth that sets people free to be who God made them to be.

Of course, most Finishers understand that there are lists that will never be finished. But a Finisher will not necessarily take a project off their list just because there has not been any progress. We all fit somewhere. Each person is an important part of God's Divine plan for how His creations function and interact on the earth.

On the other hand, when it comes to lists, Starters are known to make lists right before they go to the grocery store – and when they get to the store, they realize that they forgot their list. If a Starter has not been able to get other people involved in completing items on their list, it seems to be very easy for them to throw the list away and start a new one.

While Starters are much better at taking power naps during the day, Finishers do not require – or even enjoy – short naps to regroup and collect their mind, body, and spirit. Starters innately know to do that so they can go on about their day with new vigor and creative ability, which helps them better adjust to the tides of change and circumstances.

Sometimes Starters are labeled as being lazy for napping; in fact, it is best for their system to take power naps. By doing that, they can regroup, collect their energy, and keep from being so overstimulated that they are not able to function at their best. Typically, Starters seem to have no problem with taking short naps and still being able to fall asleep at night.

On the other hand, if Finishers try to power-nap regularly, they are likely to find themselves feeling worse and more tired – unless they have a considerable amount of time to rest. Even then, they usually do not like to take naps in the afternoon, since it makes it difficult for them to go to sleep and rest during the night. My grandmother – John's mother – was a Starter. She was able to get up in the very early morning and go to the garden and get fresh vegetables and eggs, all so she could get food ready for her family before everyone was awake. She loved doing that for the family – she was such a social Starter.

However, in the afternoon, she would also want to be in her living room listening to and laughing with her family. Many times, family members would look over to see her nodding off and napping in the middle of the day. The way she was napping looked so uncomfortable that the family would tell her she needed to go lie down and rest. But she did not want to do that, since all of the action and relational activity was going on in the living room.

Of course, the family members did not know about the foundational principles we are discussing in this book. And they sure did not know that a Starter like her just needed a safe place to close her eyes and take short naps to collect her energy, so she could keep enjoying a social life with family and friends.

Expressing how they feel is more important to Starters than stopping to analyze the facts of a situation. Most Starters like to talk in generalities, as opposed to the details that would be associated with their ideas.

In business or other teamwork, it is usually better left to the Finishers of the team to do the research on the details, and let the Starters present the concept in a charismatic way. Most Starters are good at telling stories to move people emotionally to take action. At the same time, Starters will assure others that if they trust them, everything will work out.

Abraham, who is written about in the Old Testament, is a good example of a Starter that walked by faith. He convinced many to follow him, simply because he said he heard the Word from the Lord. It is also clear in the Old Testament that the Lord is not a God that just requires blind faith. When He gave instructions to the leaders of how He wanted His house built, he gave them amazingly precise details of what He wanted.

As I pointed out before, Starters, as a whole, are more interested in developing and nurturing relationships instead of simply choosing the most efficient path. I know a lady who is willing to get on a plane and fly 800 miles, just so she can continue to see the same doctor she has been seeing for years. This Starter prefers maintaining a relationship over switching to a different, qualified doctor whose office is close to home. That may be an extreme example of my point; however, Starters, more than Finishers, innately understand that when they are in need of special treatment, loyalty will pay off well for them.

Here is another example of why it is important to have people around you who will help balance the scales of your life. My aunt worked for years with a highly-respected prosecuting attorney. When things were not going well for her, he would say, "You burn the bridges before you even get across them." Strong Finishers will want to team with Starters who can help them soothe people's wounded feelings. Teaming up will ensure that relationships can flourish over a long period of time.

The Spa Story

When it comes to some of the finer things in life, a spa is one of the ways that Finishers enjoy being alone while they meditate and think. But Starters are much more social people. If they have a hot tub, spa or jacuzzi, they prefer to sit in it and relax with someone else. Since they are so social, when they do not have a person with whom to enjoy the spa, they usually lose interest and move on to another activity.

For example, one of my friends had a beautiful spa which was built into his large deck. The problem was that his wife enjoyed working so much that he was only using the spa by himself. It was no fun for him, because there was no socialization or good conversation involved in the experience. Being in the spa was boring to him. After a while, he had the spa removed from the deck and replaced it with wood.

My dad was the same way. We had a beautiful spa at our home, but he did not want to get in the spa unless my mother got in with him. He found it boring to use the spa by himself. He, too, quit using it and replaced the spa time with a more socially interactive activity.

To balance the scales, it would be beneficial for a Finisher to get in the spa with a Starter, even though that is not really what the Finisher enjoys. As it turns out, spas are a great place to talk. What might happen is that the conversation turns to the topic of the work to be discussed. Starters like to do things with others so much that it is highly profitable for Finishers to take time to be social with them in the spa or at the table. That way, they both will be motivated to get more involved in helping to accomplish the projects that need to be done. Both sides of the energy scale will be satisfied.

I am an Enlightened Finisher, and so I love the tranquil time to meditate and enjoy the goodness of my God while sitting in the spa. However, a person like myself could become so content with that type of environment that I might miss out on so many other things in life. If

I did not have some fun and outgoing Starters around to inspire me, I might not get motivated to expand my horizons and try new, fulfilling things.

Finishers tend to be a little more uncomfortable in new social environments. Where Starters can easily start conversations with new people, Finishers generally wait for somebody to come and talk to them – unless they have a pre-planned agenda. To help balance the scales, it is appropriate – in most cases – for a Starter to make the introductions and then step away so that the Finisher can connect with others. That may leave Finishers feeling awkward at first. However, as the conversation progresses, they will be able to more freely open up and develop a relationship.

One day, at a conference, I was in an elevator with a fun and vivacious Starter business associate. While I had a couple of minutes with her, I gave her a PeopleLogics tip that she could use to be more effective in business. Within a few seconds, her dad invited himself into the conversation. I said something disarming to him, and then I walked away. My Starter wife was on the elevator as well, and could hardly believe what she just saw. She stayed behind to try to calm things down with the gentleman. Her conversation balanced the scales and countered my abruptness, which could have been taken as rudeness. She was able to soothe the gentleman and smooth out the abrasiveness that I had brought to the relationship.

In the long run, we ended up spending some time at the beach together, and he even told me that if I ever wanted a place to stay when I visited Arizona, his place was always open to me. I do not believe that the interaction would have been as smooth if my Starter wife had not stepped in. She defused the situation after I reacted to his action of interrupting me without an invitation.

Starters are amazing at keeping the relational scales balanced, which brings much more harmony to life.

Finishers are good at getting bogged down in the details – so much that it slows down the process of growth in businesses. When my father John was wanting to quickly grow his business, he would motivate my mom – a Finisher – by saying to her, "Let's just do it and get it over with." This challenge and pressure caused her to focus on the important things to be done to achieve the business goals that John had set for the business. My parents balanced each other's energy out so much that they reached the top rank in their business in a short period of time.

Starters tend to say things like, "Let's just go ahead and get started, and we can cover all of the details later." To help balance the scales, one may want to use the principles found in the words of Jesus, as recorded in *The Message*. It goes something like this: "Is there anyone here who, planning to build a new house, does not first sit down and figure the cost so you will know if you can complete the project? If you only get the foundation laid and then run out of money, you are going to look pretty foolish. People passing by will poke fun at you and say things like: "He started something he couldn't finish. He obviously did not take time to analyze the details of the cost it would take to complete the project properly, or he would have waited to actually start the project in the first place so he could enjoy the fruits of his labor when it was finished."

A visit with a banker is a great way to balance the scales with an overly optimistic Starter. The banker can help bring things into perspective and determine if a project will be feasible with the amount of money available.

In part, because Starters are flooded with so many creative ideas, they vacillate more than Finishers when following a plan. They feel it is important to give their ideas a chance to see what becomes of them. Because they like to make decisions based on feelings and on how much they like a person with whom they are doing business, Starters often overlook important details of an agreement. They also may not immediately understand the full ramifications of their decisions.

To balance the scales, it is important that Starters understand the value of the contrasting Finishers, who are more deliberate with their actions. Finishers like to think things through before they act. They move with deliberate purpose, and use structured gestures and hand motions. These characteristics are important to help Starters stay on course and not get so overly enthusiastic that they lose focus on why they started to do the project in the first place.

Because they are more optimistic about the future, Starters seem to be able to see the future with greater clarity. They can envision what it can look like when people come together to pursue a common goal. But this quality can be used for both good and bad purposes. Remember, you are becoming empowered even as you read this book. It is up to you to make sure that your motives stay pure as you use these principles to express more power and love in your life – and in the world.

When developing best-outcome models, Finishers will apply logic in order to accomplish what is best for their own lives and the world. Logic and reason are the hallmarks in the decisions that they make. Logic and reason generally seem more predictable to Finishers than the use of strong faith, feelings, and emotions. In contrast, walking by faith seems to be easier for Starters during critical decision-making moments.

Finishers are more critical of themselves than Starters, and they often labor over the thought that they could have done things better. Even if they appear to have it all together, generally, they are the ones who are the hardest on themselves. Starters, on the other hand, find it easier to say, "We learned a lot from that process. Now we can move on to our next project with greater understanding of what we should do differently." When both will acknowledge the other's point of view, they are more likely to encourage each other to move forward with a balanced approach so that the next project will not fail, but will embrace the balance of logic and faith to achieve success.

Being stuck in the past limits insightful living in the present. Starters seem to understand this easier than Finishers. It is not that Starters forget the events of the past easily; they simply try their best to leave the past behind, in order to move on and make the most out of their present and their future.

It is important for Starters to become intentional at helping Finishers let grievances with the past go and move on to better days ahead. Know up front that this is something that is not easy for Finishers to do. When Finishers are quiet and withdrawn, they have time to go over a situation in great detail in their head, pondering about what they should say next. To help them go forward, Starters will want to use open-ended questions, creatively ask what is going on with them, and encourage them to talk about the topics. Starters need to remember, however, that the Scriptures tell us, "Above all else, guard your heart." The time it takes to work through situations is worth the effort if a person believes there is value in continuing a long-term relationship with the other person.

In general, Starters come across as the more sincere type of person when communicating with others about goals and ideas. They love to connect with their people as team members with a higher calling. And now that their people are a part of a family pursuing a common vision, they will be cared for as one of their own. The founder of the Virgin brand, Richard Branson, says about his leadership style, "Train them so well that they can leave; and treat them so well that they will want to stay." Mr. Branson is a Starter.

That attitude is appealing to Finishers, since they love to use their skills and talents to complete projects that facilitate improving the human condition.

This concept does, however, lead to blurred lines when separating work and pleasure. Since Starters tend to be "all-in" kind of people, they inadvertently assume that all the people on their team are too. For example, Finishers could consider letting people know that their decision to not attend an after-work party is nothing personal. They can simply say something like, "I really appreciate the invitation, but I have something else that needs my attention at the moment," and leave it at that.

A Finisher's communication style comes across more direct and less warm to the listener than a Starter's form of communication. With that being said, if you want to get someone to get to the point quickly and get the details taken care of rapidly, you probably want to put a Finisher in charge of the project. When they direct people, they may come across overly direct and less caring; they may lose workers along the way because of this style. However, the end result is a project that is completed on or before the scheduled time.

Finishers are good listeners. When it comes to details, Finishers tend to remember – almost word for word – what was said. In contrast, Starters are prone to filter a conversation to decide what it felt like the other person was really trying to say.

A successful billionaire I know does a great job of handling his people. He casts his vision at the beginning. He lets the Finishers do the heavy lifting. Then he comes in and closes meetings and conferences with a warm and inspiring speech, which in essence puts the "whipped cream and cherry on top." Those words allow his Finishers to feel appreciated and inspired to go on and confidently start working on the next task.

Starters are the most impulsive people on the planet. Credit card companies love when Starters sign up for a new line of credit, because it offers a fun incentive when they enroll and use their card to earn points. It is very easy for Starters to get caught up in the moment and use credit to make purchases. Often, a Starter simply wants to know what the monthly payment will be, without going over the details of what the item actually costs.

One thing that can balance the scales for a couple is for them to create a prenuptial agreement that specifies that one party will not be held responsible for debt the other incurs without both partners signing off on the contract.

Business meetings often require a careful balance between the Starters and Finishers in the room. While

Finishers jump from detail to detail, bringing up points and asking questions, Starters want to see the conversation come from a broader perspective in working toward the final decisions.

As boring as it may sound to a Starter, Finishers usually do not mind keeping to themselves as they work on completing their assigned projects. Starters, on the other hand, find it almost impossible to do their best work, over a period of time, if they are not surrounded with people who boost their spirits and keep their enthusiasm high. They love to work in teams, which can be distracting to a Finisher trying to focus on pulling all the details together.

To help balance the scales and keep projects on the fast track, a Finisher should establish a deadline for the Starter group to come together and turn in their work. The Finisher should not expect the Starters to quit talking simply because they need time to complete the project. It really would be best for the Starters to remove themselves from the situation, so the Finishers can get the job finished accurately and on time. John used to regularly manage projects like this and it worked well for him.

Companies find it to be a better investment when the people that they recruit and train stay with their company for a longer period of time. Starters tend to move on from a position faster when the excitement has waned; Finishers stay with a company longer, even when it looks like the ship is sinking. Many times, it is the Finisher's persistence and tenacity that keeps a company afloat until new ideas and programs are initiated to increase profits.

When John and his wife, Tressie, were building their dream home, John could not afford to hire expensive companies to do his work. Instead, to save time and money, he hired a friend of his who knew how to run electric wires in a house. After this person – a Starter – did the electrical work, it was discovered that the wire nuts that were used for connections were not tightened properly and were coming apart.

This person had good intentions. However, he lacked the patience to make sure each wire was tightened well enough. After the discovery, John hired someone who was more detail-oriented to make sure the job was done correctly. John had not discovered and developed PeopleLogics at that time.

It may seem as though a worker is taking too much time with a job – especially if you are paying them by the hour – but it might still be a good idea to hire someone obsessed with details. In the end, you are more likely to have quality work that will stand the test of time.

When Starters feel too much pressure while on a project, they will shut down – they are unable to access their creative nature. Because of the way they are made, they need an encouraging approach, rather than a push to do too much, too fast. When asking a Starter to join a project, it is wise to tell them that they "might want to consider getting started," and then let them process how they feel about it. If too much pressure is applied too fast, they usually say no quickly and just walk away.

So, while encouragement motivates Starters, Finishers are most productive when they are pushed a bit. Finishers tend to respond well to pressure. When Finishers are pushed, they will often do more and perform better than they thought they could. For Finishers, the more that reasonable pressure is applied, the more they feel that confidence is being shown in them.

Keeping their to-do list short is not usually a very good idea. When given too few projects, Finishers tend to lose respect for their leader and then move on in favor of something more challenging.

When it comes to work, Starters will move around more quickly than Finishers, until they find something that they really enjoy, and a position they find fulfilling.

The size of the paycheck is usually not the number one thing that determines if they stay in a position. Generally, they feel that with their ease of connecting with others, they will be able to make money in a position they find enjoyable, with work that is meaningful to them.

When you hear that a certain person has a great vision for the future, you are usually talking about a Starter. A Starter's ability to cast a vision is attractive and admired by most Finishers. Finishers will be the most prone to help a leader to see that a vision comes to fruition. Again, both Starters and Finishers are needed to accomplish anything of significance.

While visiting with friends, a woman and her husband started talking to neighbors across the street. The neighbor explained that he had an idea whereby self-serve machines could be installed in airports to speed up the check-in process so travelers would enjoy a better experience while traveling. The new acquaintance liked the idea, and together this Starter and Finisher pair grew the business. It grew rapidly. Finally, a major computer corporation purchased their company. The Starter and Finisher both prospered; however, the Starter cast the vision and prospered more.

Starters want to share their ideas with others to see how it sounds to them, and to see if others think it might be good for the family or organization. On the other hand, Finishers should listen a while before giving unsolicited advice. As my one friend, a Starter, told me, "I wish Tom would just listen to my idea for at least 20 seconds before shooting it down."

Thomas Edison, the inventor of the incandescent light bulb and other amazing products, was good at finding ways to create new products. That happened in part because he was a Starter who liked to experiment with new things. Edison was also willing to keep trying until something worked well.

When a reporter once pointed out what seemed to be a complete failure on Mr. Edison's part, it is reported that Mr. Edison spoke up and said, "I have not failed – not once. I have successfully found ten thousand ways that will not work." Henry Ford, on the other hand, was a Finisher. He took an idea from another company who was already producing automobiles, and refined some production procedures. In particular, he found that he could make cars more cost-effectively by using assembly lines. Assembly lines allowed his people to do the same task over and over, so they would become skilled and efficient at doing that one activity. The assembly line process produced an automobile for the masses, at a less expensive cost than his competition.

Mr. Ford and Mr. Edison enjoyed spending winters together in Fort Myers, Florida, where they discussed and developed new ideas for their companies. If you tour Thomas Edison's winter home, you will hear how his wife did not understand why Mr. Edison took naps on his desk in the middle of the day. She arranged for a cot to be brought to his office so he could take power naps while he worked. As we have previously discussed, power-napping is a trait of a Starter, which should be embraced with your Starter colleagues if you would like to experience them at their best.

As you may imagine, I have numerous stories about how both Starters and Finishers are so important to accomplishing anything significant in the world today. The last example that I will share with you in this chapter is about how enjoyable it is to drive a convertible car in the state of Florida.

There was a time in my career that my company provided a car for me to drive. I chose a fun Sebring convertible as my desired car to drive around Florida. Florida nights are breathtaking, and I enjoy cruising around in a convertible in a major way.

I have two precious friends that I have spent much time with over the years who also lived in Florida. When I drove up in my convertible and took her for a drive, she wanted one for herself right away. She liked the style and the size. When she approached her husband about the idea he quickly said that it probably would not be that model that they would purchase. That answer caused much conflict over the ensuing weeks, because my friend felt she was missing out on the fun.

Some time went by, and her husband did his research. He determined that the Audi convertible was rated the best in that class, and he said that the Audi would be the car they would purchase. Well, my friend was not happy, especially since the Audi had less legroom for back seat passengers. But they did end up purchasing the Audi convertible, and that settled the issue to the husband's liking.

Later, it was discovered that the Sebring model that I was enjoying had a poorly-designed engine; my engine quit at 45,000 miles. This is virtually unheard of with a new car that only had one owner. My friend's Audi, on the other hand, lasted years longer than the Sebring that I drove.

You can see that it is beneficial for each side of the relationship to take a breath and consider the value that the other person is bringing to the table.

To balance the scales, all of the traits of Starters and Finishers need to be understood and appreciated.

When working together, the more we can embrace one another's God-given energy, and the more happy and unified we will be. Let us keep going, and we will talk about how we are made and what we can – or cannot – do about it.

CHAPTER 5

How We Were Made

One of the reasons that the world is filled with excessive amounts of conflict is because most people do not understand the principles we will discuss in this chapter.

When I was growing up, I wanted to be like my dad. He was such an inspiration, and had a fun and charismatic way about him. As you read on, you will discover why I never achieved my desire to have that same kind of charisma – and why you may not have achieved your desire to be like one of your parents or friends.

Because I did not understand the principle of how we are created, I felt inferior in many ways. Consequently, I could not focus on what I was designed to do.

And actually, I was not designed to be like my dad – I was created with the opposite energy type of my father. This design is in place so people like my dad and

I could work and play together, complementing each other's energy.

Everyone has strengths and weaknesses. Just because you and your mother are both females, or you and your father are both males, does not mean that you were made to behave alike. One's energy strength makes up the difference that the other person's weakness brings to the relationship – in essence, achieving a balance of nature.

Mary, the mother of Jesus of Nazareth, knew what she was getting when she had her baby. We, too, can now know what we are getting from God when we have a child or grandchild. We can also be better equipped to bring them up in a way that is best suited for how God made them and for their function on earth.

One size does not fit all. Just because a parent has a baby boy does not mean he is going to have the same energy as his father. Quite the opposite is usually true. That baby boy gets his energy from his mother's father. It is all designed by God so there is a balance of nature and energy between biological fathers and sons.

This concept plays out when people are having a family gathering. For the most part, the women congregate in the kitchen together. Since God designed the energy of mothers and daughters to complement each other, it makes sense that mothers and daughters would be made with opposite types of energy.

Although the example above is common in most cultures, it is the energy type that ultimately determines with whom people enjoy working over a long period of time.

Although children of the same DNA can act very differently, I have noticed that because of family pride, parents want to say things like, "She is so much like me it's not even funny." Or, "He is just a chip off the old block." "Like father, like son" is rarely the case when we are talking about the energy of fathers and their biological children.

Yes – keep in mind that PeopleLogics training is based on actual biological parents and siblings. We have run into situations where there were questions about why the energy was not balanced, when the children were adopted and they did not know this was the case.

With sons, the energy flows from their mother's father, through their mother, and then on to them. Most everyone in the birthing room knows who actually gave birth to the son. So, it is fairly easy to know what energy type the son embodies, once it is known who the mother's biological father is, and what his energy type is.

This is one of the reasons there are so many mother-in-law jokes. The energy type of the mother-in-law and the son-in-law are almost always similar. Many times, this situation causes the two to repel each other as they jockey for positions of power and influence. This is especially true with Finishers.

It is important, if at all possible, to allow one's daughter to spend time with her father's mother. These two energy types are some of the most alike on the planet – just as a son's energy type is derived from his mother's father.

When a person understands the type of child that God has given them, or is going to give them – and what kind of energy they have – they will be much better equipped to be effective parents and grandparents.

Now we can stop experimenting with what we think may or may not work, and follow God's divine design when raising our children. Using PeopleLogics principles, we can equip them for what they are best suited. Understanding energy types helps us to understand where our children are most likely to excel – and that extends to evaluating the type of life partner that would provide them the most potential for success.

We can also make a difference in the lives of parents by taking some of the guesswork out of understanding how they should nurture and train their children. We can have a whole new generation of parents who will be able to know the kind of energy that their precious children will have, right from the start.

CHAPTER 6

Embracing Energy in Relationships

There are many types of relationships, including those that are intimate, those that are friendships, and workplace relationships. In this chapter, we will focus on personal relationships; we will cover those in the workplace more in Chapter 8. It is important for us to seek healthy, fulfilling relationships that enhance our well-being.

It is possible to be attracted to someone, but due to a lack of energy compatibility, nothing ever happens with the other person. For example, when I was starting my third year of high school, I changed schools. That meant meeting new people and making new friends. After getting my locker and class schedule, I noticed a girl getting into her locker down the hall from me. I had to walk right past her every day to get to classes. As the year progressed, I would say "hi" from time to time, and occasionally flirt with her. I really liked the way she looked, but I could tell there were no real sparks between us. I was perplexed by that for a long time.

Later I learned about PeopleLogics and understood the reason that nothing ever happened between us. We were both Finishers with linear energy. These identical energy types will not enjoy deep emotional chemistry or an attraction that will last. Years later, when I went to a class reunion and saw her again, she was married to a Starter.

People frustrated in their personal relationships may want to look at their own energy type, as well as their partners, to determine if it is going to be worth the time, effort, and resources, to continue their relationship. Most successful relationships are made up of a Starter and a Finisher.

Unlike my father John Goetz, who was married for more than 40 years, I was more like the Connor Mead character in Matthew McConaughey's movie, *Ghosts of Girlfriends Past*. I had many girlfriends. Some were Starters and some were Finishers.

There is a stark contrast in how their emotions become evident in intimate relationships. How each type gives and receives affection is quite different and is affected by their energy.

When Finishers are involved in a heated argument and get hurt, they tend to withdraw, as they hold in much of their anger. This can result in the Finisher exploding over some seemingly trivial situation later – while the real issue is still hidden under the surface, unresolved. We find the solution in the Scriptures, in a passage known as the love chapter. In this passage – I Corinthians 13 – it says that love holds no record of wrongs. However, for that to play out, a Finisher has to become very intentional.

When it comes to love, the most passionate people on the planet are Starters. If you are looking for a huggy-kissy kind of person, look for a Starter. Their desire for physical touch, and deep physical intimacy, is like a trademark for them. But when it comes to diving deeper into a personal relationship, this passion can drive them into making some seemingly silly decisions when it comes to choosing a partner.

Finishers love to be pursued – to the point that it almost exhausts the Starters who are interested in having a personal relationship with them. Generally, Starters are much better at opening the door to intimacy and finding who they want to be with in a personal relationship.

More steady and calculating in their thinking and decision-making processes, Finishers will fully invest in a relationship once he or she makes the decision to commit. Then, the Finisher will tend to take control of the relationship and try to make it work for a long period of time. Although they can seem more distant or unemotional, the Finisher provides stability when the energy of the Starter wanes.

A Finisher embraces their ability to remain at a more stable emotional level; they do not need naps to regain energy in the afternoon. They make good fiduciary "gatekeepers" when handling finances and budgeting. They are more practical when starting a new relationship adventure.

So they do not get internally overstimulated, Starters prefer quieter, softer music. Quieter music will not raise their energy level abruptly. Finishers, on the other hand, usually enjoy louder, high-energy music which helps raise their energy level quicker to their level of preference. And, they prefer music with a good beat and rhythm over one with primarily strong lyrics. High energy in music energizes and excites Finishers.

When I first started dating my wife – a brand-new, passionate relationship – we went to a restaurant down by a river. We enjoyed each other's company so much that we closed down the restaurant. We needed to leave, so went outside to sit on a bench.

As we were making out, Laura became annoyed right in the middle of our romantic moment. People in a parking lot, which was some distance away, were playing loud music. It overstimulated and frustrated her. On the other hand, for me, as an enlightened Finisher, it was exciting – an addition to the moment – but we left the place because it became too much for her. To this day, both music volume and music choice are areas where we practice understanding. We try to embrace a happy medium regarding music.

Allowing that Finishers take longer to recover from a conflict, the Starter partner would benefit from giving the Finisher more time and space to process their emotions.

One day I was listening to a pastor, and he was describing how this very issue was playing out in his personal relationship. He and his wife would have heated agreements and discussions. But after he believed they had reached a reasonable resolution, and things seemed back to normal, he would ask her if she wanted to go get something to eat. She would say, "Oh no. It is not that easy." This is an example of how the lack of understanding about energy differences is so prevalent.

This was a public Starter figure telling his story, but he had no real answers about why it happens regularly. He had no idea what to do differently when it continued to occur.

When my dad, John Goetz, was given the message of PeopleLogics and all of the insights that come with it, he was talking with a friend about "getting it out." He said, "I can't do it without Nathan. He's the one who is going to help me pull it together and get it out." That was a clear example of a Starter (my dad) wanting and needing a Finisher (me) to implement a project within the structure of a very personal relationship.

Dr. Martin Luther King Jr. is an example of a Starter who was not initially looking for a position of leadership in the civil rights movement. Once he was recruited, however, the issue became very personal to him. And because he was a Starter with the ability to move people to embrace the concept of equality for all, his "I Have A Dream" speech inspired people all over the nation to take action. The speech is still remembered to this day by a massive number of people as the moment when the tides of racism shifted.

When a Starter is moved emotionally – as was Dr. King – you have all of them or almost none of them. It is not wise to expect someone like Dr. King to inspire the masses and then take care of all the seemingly small details of his life. No matter how great or small a person is, they have a personal life. In the case of someone like Dr. King, he was surrounded by willing and able Finishers who did not seek the limelight but believed in the cause. They were willing to facilitate and protect the energy of this passionate man. The more that Finishers understand that their strengths are necessary to support those with tremendous passions and visions, the quicker that objectives can be accomplished.

In a small Texas town, a minister by the name of John Osteen decided, with a small group of people, to start a church in a dusty, abandoned feed store. As with most Starters, he did not mind starting small while following his passion. Later, Lakewood Church grew in size, and his son Joel enjoyed working in the video suite to help make his dad look good as he ministered on television. As the story goes, there came a day that John Osteen started asking Joel to get on stage to preach. Joel says that he recalled his dad asking him over and over to deliver a message from the stage until, one day, Joel finally said yes. Shortly after that, John Osteen passed, and Joel was pushed into the limelight, ministering from the stage each week.

But as the church grew, there was still something missing. Joel knew that he did not have the same skills as Victoria, his Starter wife. As Joel tells it, one day he said to Victoria that she should get up and start "speaking faith" into the people. According to Joel, the church doubled in size after she started "speaking faith" to the congregation each week. Joel went on to become known as "America's Pastor." The moral of the story is: when partners drop their egos and embrace their differences, much more can be accomplished – with less strife.

Ronald Reagan was an American actor who became the president of the United States. However, the person who helped him discover his place in the arena of politics is said to be his Finisher wife, Nancy. It was after he began his relationship with Nancy that he switched political parties and ended up in the most famous house in the United States – the White House. Like Dr. King, the president is famous for speaking just a few words that changed the course of human history. Words said with the passion for which Starters are known can move mountains; in the case of President Reagan, those words were, "Mr. Gorbachev, tear down this wall." The wall did come down and Germany has remained united to this day.

Nancy Reagan was a beautiful, refined individual who did not need to be the center of attention to know her value in the relationship. Her value was keeping President Reagan from going "off the rails." She kept him from becoming too extreme and comforted him when he was down.

The famous Starter talk show host Oprah Winfrey embraced and shared her energy style with a very simple list called "Oprah's Favorite Things." Oprah could afford to give major gifts to her audience; but Starters seem to naturally understand that it does not take major gestures to make people feel special. So, more than once, she chose to give a product called Basic-H2 to her audience as one of her favorite things. Keep in mind that this product is very inexpensive – yet, as a Starter, she remained in touch with the simple things in life like the importance of getting a stain out of a carpet.

Whether or not you like this next person I will mention, the odds are that he will be in the history books for a long time to come. Donald Trump decided to run for the U.S. president's office without ever having run previously for any political office. "The Donald," as some people like to call him, was a bit of a wild card. When my wife asked me if I had heard that Donald Trump was running for office, I immediately said, "Well, I don't know whether he is going to win or not, but he sure is going to make things interesting." He is a Starter; his wives, on the other hand, have been Finishers. Even one of his chief spiritual consultants was a female Finisher. The PeopleLogics system helps one understand how a person like Paula White, who used to live on government cheese in Florida, could ascend to such a high advisory position. The valuable takeaway should be: if you are a Finisher, find your Starter – and if you are a Starter, find your Finisher.

Wise Finishers, once they find their Starter, know that it is important to guard their tongue and let them tell stories – even if you have heard the story 28 times – so they can solidify their thoughts before deciding how to move forward on a life decision. One of the things John Goetz would say about his wife was, "Right or wrong, Tressie knows how to make a decision."

Knowing that Starters tend to exaggerate when telling stories, it is also important to not shut down a Starter's flow as they arrive at an important point in their narrative. Taking this to an extreme does happen. For example, I heard about a female sales trainer who said to her audience, "Don't let the facts get in the way of a good story."

If you go into a relationship with a Starter, know that you are probably going to have to clarify many verbal messes made by them in off-the-cuff conversations, or when they go off-script. Starters are great at what they do, but fact-checking every word they say is not their strength. For example, President of the United States Joe Biden, a Starter, while going off-script and sharing his personal feelings on the world stage, said, "This man (meaning Vladimir Putin, president of Russia) cannot remain in power." Those comments ran opposite to current United States foreign policy, and President Biden's staff started walking back the comments right away. The staff of President Donald Trump had this same difficulty. They regularly had to clarify statements that President Trump made while not reading the teleprompter. Starters need Finishers to help clarify the message and the position of their organization.

CHAPTER 7

Resolving Conflict in Relationships

Time Conflict Resolution

There is a lot of conflict over time management between Starters and Finishers. One person says to another, "You are always running late; I want to be early to get a good seat." The other may say, "We have plenty of time to get to that event." Typically, neither Starters nor Finishers understand the other's internal desires when it comes to time.

Why are Starters late so often? Starters are usually having so much fun at what they are already doing that they do not seem to consider how long it will take to prepare to arrive on time. This is especially true if they are expected to be on time to the minute.

The real issue is that they prefer the energy level in the room to be high enough for them to walk in and not feel a letdown. If they are allowed an extra few minutes, the evening will go much better for them. If they can come in with things already in motion, the energy level will be higher. It is not that a Starter cannot be trained to be on time to the minute; it is just that a Starter is feelings-oriented. Relationships are more important to them than the clock.

Starters perform at their best when they can ride in on the energy that others have already created. They can come in with their creative juices flowing and then dazzle the audience. It is the reverse when the event is over. They typically want to get out before all the energy has left the building. Starters feel very uncomfortable if they arrive early, and they usually feel the same way if they cannot leave the event before most everyone has left.

In contrast, when Finishers set a time to be someplace, they usually see it as a goal that must be reached. For the most part, they feel like a failure if they do not arrive on time or a little early. Finishers are task-oriented, so it only makes sense that they would make arriving on time a task that needs to be completed correctly.

Since Starters are so relationship-oriented, they tend to think, "What is a few extra minutes between friends?"

Having the opportunity to get together with others is more important to them than being somewhere at a set time.

Someone I was talking with the other day gave me an example of how this kind of conflict played out in her life. When she was growing up, her brother had a car and she did not. He would say, "I will be leaving for school at 7:30 a.m., and if you are not ready, I am leaving without you." Sure enough, if she was even one minute late, he would leave her behind without saying a word. He was a Finisher who was not flexible, and when he set a time to leave, that personal commitment was more important than accommodating his Starter sister.

My own family also had a major lack of understanding in this area. I can not tell you how many Sundays went by when my mother and I would be out in the car, ready for church and honking the horn, waiting for my dad so we could leave and not arrive late.

Later in life, after starting to understand PeopleLogics, my dad and I had a conversation about this topic, as it related to his church. He told me that he had never understood the conflict, since there were people at the church to unlock the doors and get things started. I had no idea this was the case; my priority had been the clock, but his responsibilities did not require him to be there early, or even on time.

When people first start dating, the conflict about time may not be very apparent to both partners. Most often, people tend to overlook those differences and are happy to just be with each other. Typically, however, the Starter is unaware that the Finisher has started making a mental list of things about their partner that they plan to change once they get married. Later, when the two do marry, little things suddenly become major issues – especially issues dealing with time. Finishers can become openly angry when they think Starters are loafing around, especially when the Starter is consistently late.

For example, when a Starter is preparing to go somewhere, they may initially motivate the Finisher to begin getting ready. The Finisher focuses, gets the job done, and is ready to leave on time. In contrast, while that is taking place, the Starter may still be checking emails or chatting with a friend that just called. The Starter may feel that those are necessary steps to take before leaving, while the Finisher may see them as activities that waste time or are low-priority. The Finisher may be thinking, "Why did you keep asking me over and over if I was ready to leave, when you are not ready yourself?" Then a conflict over time ensues.

If the Starters are leading the event, they may be more prone to alter their behavior and aim to be on time. Nevertheless, it usually is like a mad rush for them to pull themselves and their children together, if they have any, so they can be remotely close to being on time.

I am reminded of a famous lady in the Christian world of ministry who would draw very large crowds to her meetings. She was a Starter, and would make her grand entrance by saying, "Have you been waiting on meeee?"

Music Style Differences

When I was growing up, one of the conflicts with my dad, John, was a lack of understanding about music choices. Even though my dad was very tolerant about the type of music I purchased, whenever I wanted to play rock music, things did not go well. He liked the kind of music where he could understand every word, even if the recording was poorly produced. Referring to my taste for rock, he asked, "Why do you like that kind of music? You can't even understand the words." I replied that for me, the appeal was not so much the words but the great beat.

We have already said that a Finisher has linear energy and that it takes more stimulus to raise their energy level. Therefore, high energy in music is very important in order for Finishers to get excited and motivated. My dad, on the other hand, was a Starter; and the Starter's energy spikes more easily. They are easily overstimulated, which means that any loud guitar riff, particularly from an electric guitar, would send his emotions through the roof! So, music preference was a chief conflict between us. Understanding music styles, including volume levels, is very important to making any relationship work.

In the previous chapter, I told the story of an early date with my wife, Laura. Another example of energy differences came when we were looking forward to our anniversary. I was amazed that the rock group, Boston, was performing a concert on our anniversary date. I asked her if she knew of Boston. She said, "no," so I played her one of their ballads. She said, "Oh, that's good music. I would like to go to that concert after dinner – excellent idea."

At the show, it turned out that the song I played for her was the mellowest song of the evening. Sometime in the middle of the concert, she got up and left. I did not understand where she went, and why she was away so long. I found out that she had gone to the restroom to get away from the loud electric guitar sounds – she said later that it was "horrific." She could not leave the building because the venue would not allow her to come back into the building after exiting. She finally returned to her seat, but we left the concert to get away from the noise that was overstimulating her.

The tendency for loud, high-energy music to cause overstimulation in Starters is likely the reason why most country music, jazz, and other calmer forms of music are so popular with Starters in the United States. Starters generally prefer music with easy-to-understand words, less stimulating instrumentation, and lower volume.

As a teenager, my dad took me to a concert that he felt would expose me to the type of music that he liked. Jimmy Swaggart, a well-known international Christian evangelist, attracted large crowds and I was intrigued as to why the place was packed. Since I loved music so much and played the drums since I was a little boy, I was interested in hearing Jimmy sing and play the piano. In the middle of playing Southern gospel music, he stopped and made a passionate point. He said, "The Christian rock music that they are playing today is of the devil." He too was singing Christian music – but he was referring to other bands of that time who were singing louder, higher-energy Christian music with similar messages. Those sounds disturbed Jimmy's Starter nervous system.

As a Finisher, I liked that kind of high energy – it raised my level of excitement. Looking back, I now understand it overstimulated Jimmy and his sensory system to the point that he literally felt like it was "of the devil." Even though it was Christian music, he could not understand how it could be a good thing.

I was also taught that when having a party, one should start the music light, and then slowly turn the volume up as the evening progresses. That way, the energy level would gradually increase and people would have more fun. That scenario is great for Finishers. However, Starters do not like the sound so loud that they cannot have a peaceful conversation. They are usually the ones that are asking someone to turn down the music – or they ask others to leave with them to talk in a quieter environment. So, once again, to embrace the energy is to know that Starters want music that does not overstimulate them.

Communication Style Differences

Words are important, and more so to Finishers. Finishers weigh their words carefully, so they presume that others have done the same.

Although Starters need a safe place to air their thoughts and vent their emotions, it is not a good choice for them to express themselves in front of unenlightened Finishers who are close to the situation. Finishers who do not understand these PeopleLogics principles do not know that Starters speak to hear themselves think. We know that once we speak, we can not put words back in our mouths. Therefore, it is wise to remember that what Starters say around Finishers may be misconstrued if they do not understand the communication style. Finishers can become defensive and jump to the wrong conclusion – that a Starter's comments were carefully considered before they were spoken.

When considering their options, Finishers will over-analyze things more than Starters. To help resolve conflict, it is helpful for both to understand that it is easier to get Starters excited about an idea, while it is best to narrow down the options for Finishers to two or three so they can dive in and make informed decisions quicker.

Generally, Starters get over conflicts and disagreements and move on much faster than Finishers. Finishers do not get over conflict easily, and will sometimes wait to bring up the conflict until later. That can allow disagreeable feelings to build up and surface at an inopportune time. The Finisher may explode over some seemingly trivial situation – while the real issue seems unresolved. Starters will be caught off guard wondering why an old conflict has come up, because the situation happened years ago. It would be wise for Starters to anticipate that this is going to happen regularly with Finishers. Likewise, Finishers will need to become very intentional to be able to forgive and move on quickly.

The principles of PeopleLogics work. People have to want to know – and learn – and use them to produce harmony even though it may seem foreign to their way of thinking.

One situation I deal with regularly is when both Starters and Finishers believe that they are going to change the other person, and are not willing to love and understand them. They do not want to adapt to the other person's desires and needs.

The world is made up of givers and takers. If a person is not open to becoming a giver – and prefer their partner to be – the relationship will not progress in a healthy manner, even if they take time to study and learn PeopleLogics principles.

The Scriptures state that it is more blessed to give than it is to receive. If one's mindset becomes a passion to give, versus a passion to take, the world will relationally become a better place.

The Wise Starter

People who do not understand the principles of PeopleLogics may say that Starters just talk in circles. A wise Starter waits until the time is right, and they feel good about the situation – and the other person feels good about them. Then, they are able to ask the other person to go with them to the next step, whatever that may be – and usually by that time, the person is ready to say yes.

Even if they say no, the Starter still instinctively will be fine with that, and will take the response as no big deal – nothing that they cannot overcome. A wise Starter knows that they also need a safe place to share ideas without being pushed too hard for answers. They need time to ponder the details of the situation. When they are given the needed time and space, they are better able to continue to talk to the person in a friendly manner about all of the other topics of interest.

Generally, the Starter will continue to talk about seemingly small concepts until they believe the person with whom they are talking begins to like them more as a person. The Starter will feel like it is OK to keep exploring ideas with this individual. They may think, *This person probably does know what they are talking about, and I like them. They make me feel good about them. Maybe I should at least consider taking action on their suggestions.*

When Starters get overwhelmed, they can get a bit mouthy. Although they do not intend to, it just kind of happens. When too many things happen at once, they feel overwhelmed and can use words in a seemingly destructive manner. Fortunately, they are also the ones who are quick to initiate positive dialogue, which quickly helps bring the relationship back in line. This generally happens sooner than Finishers want to forgive the Starters and are willing to go back to a harmonious relationship.

If how you are communicating in your relationships is not working for you, it may be time to apply the PeopleLogics training to improve your life.

The Wise Finisher

A wise Finisher is one who takes time to listen to all of a Starter's ideas before saying no to a project. Because Starters need a safe place to think out loud and process their thoughts and feelings, a Finisher will want to be careful about implementing an idea too soon, or shutting the Starter down before they are finished expressing their complete idea.

We have already discussed how Starters like to talk and share their vision of what something could be like in the future – and that they can be perceived to be less logical and more expressive than Finishers. This is how God made them; so it is best to know that when we are listening to Starters, they exaggerate while telling stories. Again, they communicate in a way that focuses on feelings over facts.

Financial Conflict Resolution

One of the best things a couple can do is have regular budget meetings – not catastrophe meetings – budget meetings. This is a time when the couple can come together, assess the past, and plan for the future.

For most couples, this is hard to do on a regular basis. That is why it is important to have a trainer cover this topic with you so that little things do not become big issues. Here is an example of good communication regarding a budget. My friend who fought in World War II sent his checks home to his wife while he was serving abroad. Every month, she would give him a list of expenditures to account for every dollar that was spent. But in most relationships, finances are not discussed with any regularity. So when Starters – who tend to spend money spontaneously – come head-to-head with Finishers – who tend to be nitpicky about small budgetary items – conflict may result.

To the best of my knowledge, money and sex are the two biggest issues that cause conflict in personal relationships; therefore, they are two primary areas of focus if we want healthy connections.

As John and I studied and trained people, we found that encouraging monthly financial meetings for couples led to more harmonious personal relationships. A desire to come together and discuss financial issues before they become a source of conflict is vital. And, maintaining financial accountability is the best way to address conflicts concerning money in a relationship. If you have difficulty discussing finances as a couple, it may be necessary to involve a third party for success in this area – someone who is not part of your family. People join fitness centers and hire personal trainers for their body; but rarely do they have meetings with a trainer to help them with their finances. Wealth management is important at every level. Our past does not have to equal our future.

What does not work well is to rapidly spend money just because you have a credit line – and get points for free things based on your spending. When the bills pile up, it will lead to major conflicts in your relationship.

Remember, money and sex are the two things that cause the most conflict in a relationship. In most cases, when only one person in a relationship is dictating the finances, what happens in the bedroom activities will deteriorate as well. A balance of power is vital if people expect relationships to thrive. Although there is often a head of a home or business organization, there are very few people who desire to live or work with a dictator.

It may be wise to seek financial counseling before marriage. A simple financial formula that many wildly successful people follow is the 10/20/70 rule. The formula teaches that the first 10 percent goes to God and His work. Partnering with God is the best thing one can ever do for a business or personal relationship. It also tells the universe, and your subconscious, that there is plenty to go around. This action releases our mind to leave the belief system of lack and that "there is not enough," and it opens our mind to attract opportunities, finances and promotions. It also prepares us to be ready to recognize opportunities when they arise.

The next 20 percent goes to investments and savings. Generally, this is where a lot of Starters have difficulty, due to the fact they like to spend more than they have. It is clear, however, that the majority of personal bankruptcies in the world are caused by spontaneous purchases for nonessential items.

The next 70 percent is what a person uses for daily life. Go have some fun. Enjoy the fruits of your labor, and care for your household. When one partner comes to an agreement with the other person – or even themselves – about how to spend the money, it works. Even though a

Starter can have a tendency to spontaneously spend too much, Finishers can over-analyze even small purchases. Both sides are capable of dysfunctional behaviors, but there is a middle ground. Now that you have discovered the roots of the behaviors, it is easier to address the tendencies of each type of energy, and discover a balance of nature that will produce more harmony in the relationship.

CHAPTER 8

PeopleLogics in the Workplace

Management Styles

"Fun is one of the most important – and underrated – ingredients in any successful venture. If you're not having fun, then it's probably time to call it quits and try something else."

SIR RICHARD BRANSON

"I'm here to build something for the long-term. Anything else is a distraction."

MARK ZUCKERBERG

Sir Richard Branson is a Starter who states in his book, *The Virgin Way,* that he dropped out of the prestigious Stowe School when he was 16 because he could not understand how sitting inside the four walls of that classroom was relevant to his future. After leaving school, he went on to start his first venture, *Student* magazine.

In the preface of his book, he goes on to say that he has borderline ADD (attention deficit disorder). His description of himself is interesting; many Starters are told that they have ADD simply because they were not designed to focus on a specific topic as long as Finishers do. They enjoy starting projects and turning them over to someone else to take care of the details after they get excited about a new venture. Richard Branson now has around 400 companies under his Virgin brand, which includes his current venture – promoting space tourism.

He says in his book that there are many things that can be learned by listening intently to everyone, not just to the self-professed experts. He says that perhaps the most important thing is to have fun. Starter bosses like Branson are willing to risk generating unpredictable consequences in pursuit of an enjoyable outcome.

One of the ways we can tell if a person like Richard Branson is a Starter is by learning more about his mother. As Richard describes her, Eve Branson was a human whirlwind who regularly jumped on the latest big thing to develop an enterprise out of it. He also says that he was blessed with an indomitable spirit that unquestionably came from his mother's side of the family. Knowing what you have learned so far, it is easy to understand that Branson's energy type would have undoubtedly come from his mother and her side of the family.

Encouragement Versus Being Pushed

Whether a person is working their way up in an organization or leading a team, identifying and understanding the principles of PeopleLogics will surely give them an advantage in working with others to reach their goals.

There is a tremendous amount of conflict in the business world because of the approaches people use when they are trying to get people involved in a project. When a Starter feels pushed by someone to be a part of an activity or business opportunity, they tend to shut down and withdraw from being involved in the project. It is as if their brains go into overload and they back off from all of the stimulation and pressure.

On the other hand, Finishers enjoy a challenge and appreciate the faith a person puts in them. They believe they are capable of handling a difficult task without a problem and agree to get involved. When a Finisher does not feel challenged, they usually fade away and find something more demanding.

To help resolve conflict, it is important to know how to guide a conversation while recruiting a Starter to get involved. The word "might" can become the best word to use when approaching a Starter with an idea. To say, "You **might** want to. . ." can be beneficial when persuading a Starter to involve themselves in a worthwhile or profitable cause.

Overall, Starters respond well to encouragement; and again, they do not like feeling pushed or severely challenged when they are asked to take action or make a quick decision. Using the word "might" is beneficial, in that it gives Starters the time and space to process their options and commitment level. In contrast, Finishers think people have more faith in them if they are given projects that push them to their very limit. They perform well under pressure to get projects finished on time.

It Seemed Like a Good Idea

The following is a story that provides a bit of a history lesson. It highlights the importance of admitting when one makes a mistake – and then quickly changing course. You may not be the CEO of a company as large as Coca-

Cola. However, you are probably a leader to someone. The following Coca-Cola formula-change story can be found on their website, coca-colacompany.com:

On April 23, 1985, the Coca-Cola Company announced it was changing the formula for the world's most popular soft drink, spawning consumer angst across the nation. They introduced reformulated Coca-Cola, calling it "new Coke," and marking the first formula change in 99 years. The company did not set out to create the firestorm of consumer protest that ensued. The change came about because consumer preference for Coca-Cola was dipping, as was consumer awareness. That changed, of course, in the summer of 1985, as the consumer outcry over "new Coke" was replaced by consumer affection for Coca-Cola Classic. Consumers started hoarding the "old" Coke and there were calls of protests by the thousands. By June 1985, the company was getting 1,500 calls a day on its consumer hotline, compared with 300 a day before the taste change. People seemed to hold any Coca-Cola employee – from security officers at our headquarters building to their neighbors who worked for Coke – personally responsible for the change. The CEO received a letter addressed to "Chief Dodo, The Coca-Cola Company." (He often said he was more upset that it was actually delivered to him!) Another person wrote to him asking for his autograph – because, in years to come, the signature of "one of the dumbest executives in American business history" would be worth a fortune. Suddenly everyone was talking about Coca-Cola, realizing what an important role it played in his or her life.

That July, the story that the "old" Coca-Cola was returning to the store shelves as Coca-Cola Classic led to network newscasts and made the front page of virtually every major newspaper. Consumers applauded the decision. In just two days after the announcement of the Coca-Cola Classic, the Coca-Cola Company received 31,600 telephone calls on the hotline. Coca-Cola was obviously more than just a soft drink.

The moral of the story is: when one makes a bad decision, it is best to admit it and change course quickly. It is not wise to try to make the plan work to save face or your ego. For everyone's sake, admit you judged the situation wrongly and make the changes necessary to get back on course. Doing this is generally easier for

Starters. It is the Finishers who are more prone to dig in their heels, and become determined to make their decisions work.

Nonverbal Cues

Starters tend to be outstanding at reading people's body language and nonverbal communication. The dysfunctional side of this ability is illustrated by what often happens when a Starter is having a discussion with another person while driving. The Starter is driving down the road, but they look over repeatedly at their passenger while they are telling a story. They are looking at the other person's facial expressions and body language instead of paying attention to the traffic. Most of the time this will continue to happen with a Starter, even if the other person makes it clear that they can hear just fine and asks them to "please watch the road."

Knowing that this will continue to happen, it is a good idea to make eye contact with a Starter driver from time to time while being a copilot – watching the road and traffic with them at the same time, whether on business or pleasure.

Expectations

Finishers usually have more unspoken expectations than do Starters. Starters are generally more transparent about who they are and what they want out of life. However, Starters are known to be able to change course quickly once another interesting opportunity or idea surfaces.

Also, since Finishers are efficient communicators, they can try to close deals too quickly. This tends to make Starters extremely uncomfortable – and even defensive – since, in their minds, the relationship has not gone through the appropriate phases. When this happens, Finishers can come across a bit cold and insensitive to Starters, which may cause the Starter to step back. Finishers find security when Starters explain their vision and remain part of the process.

Starters will want to become aware of the fact that there is a time to stop talking and to start writing. There is a time to stop chatting and talking about a project and a time to decide what to do next.

Starters are so good at going through the starting process properly that they tend to not know when it is time to close the deal. It is good to have a Finisher function as the closer, so they can answer detailed questions and support the person who is "selling the sizzle."

In business and in life, once a deal is settled, Starters need a support team around them who will administer the accounts and provide customer service.

Many times, Starters will come up with an idea and throw out enough content that the Finisher will be prompted to start planning the details in order to effectively implement the idea. The Finisher then takes over the administration of the project at hand. They may even feel at liberty to create a time management schedule for the project. However, Starters may still want more time to develop a relationship with the person with whom they are engaged before they close the deal.

Unless the relationships have become personal, Starters are less likely to enjoy following up with people. They like getting people enthused about the project and "getting the order." However, they usually want somebody else to follow up with the administrative side of the relationships. If a Starter does follow up, you can rest assured that there will be a great deal of personal content in their conversations.

Starters may not care to handle the follow-ups themselves, but they do like to make sure it gets done. They like the security of having Finishers around them to take care of these details. It is not that they believe that they are superior and more important than the Finishers in the room. Starters just usually know that they are not designed to do the repetitive items very well.

If expected to do repetitive jobs for a long period of time, Starters often get bored. Following up on mailing lists in an office cubicle or addressing a customer's detailed concerns is not fulfilling to most Starters. Their energy type is not designed for continually processing the details. As my publisher, a Starter, likes to say, "I do not work in the weeds." She is amazing at leading a team. However, she relies on Finishers like my editor to get the details right.

It is generally true that Starters are better at going out and getting accounts and moving the masses. If you want to save face with a client and keep them from leaving your company, you might want to send out a Starter.

If a frustrated client has not had their expectations met or feels they were not treated properly, send a Starter. Starters are much better at listening to others' feelings on an emotional level and making an individual feel good about what the company can do for them. However, the day-to-day administrative side of production is best suited for a Finisher.

To illustrate that point, here is a story set in a dentist's office. In the United States, a dentist's office needs to schedule and follow up with patients every six months, so patients will continue to make dental hygiene a priority. Follow-up is now being handled by electronic means in most developing countries after the appointment is booked, because the personal touch is not needed until the patient arrives at the office. However, when the patient arrives, it is best that they are greeted by a Starter receptionist. It is beneficial if the receptionist has a warm personality and makes the patient feel valued. To get a premium for services, the office staff should have the ability to put patients at ease before putting them in a chair to get work done – work that is usually not very enjoyable.

Currently, I go to a dentist in Naples, Florida. When I first called the receptionist, she was warm and kind, which made me feel good about doing business with this dental practice. And when I arrived for my appointment, the young lady at the desk had a fun personality and made me feel right at home. I knew that this office charged more than the office that I had used before, but that did not seem to matter to me. I was happy to be there, and felt confident that I would be treated more like someone with feelings than I was at my former dental office. The receptionist was a Starter.

Later in the process, it was time to pay my bill. The Starter receptionist, again, knew how to make the process warm and enjoyable. She asked pleasantly, "Would you like to pay the full amount today?" instead of saying, "Today you owe. . ." Both of us knew quite well that I would not be leaving the office without paying my bill; yet, her projecting a warm, caring attitude during the transaction made it easier for me to pay extra for the outstanding service. Even when she revealed the exorbitant amount of the bill, she smiled. She never went into the cold hard facts of the matter – that I needed to pay the bill so she could move on to her next patient. So, when at all possible, it is best to have a Starter on the front end of the process, making people feel warm and welcome as they are about to get their services.

Because Finishers tend to be more structured than Starters, it is important to give Finishers a detailed job description. Only then are they able to get comfortable with what is expected of them, and they will be able to excel in their assigned role within the organization.

Finishers are able to feel good about their achievements when they know the company's specific goals with clients. Once there is a clear structure in place and they know that they are doing a good job, they will perform above and beyond the expectations assigned to them. A Finisher will become frustrated when they are given last-minute tasks, or if the tasks are presented to them in a disorderly fashion. They thrive much better in a structured environment. They are confident in their ability to administer any project more efficiently when given information that is organized and on time.

Starters love to meet people face to face. Even though we have technology that makes it unnecessary to travel to meet someone face to face, Starters still enjoy the meetings. They find it more fulfilling to see someone in person to connect at a deeper level while conducting business. Video conferencing also helps facilitate that desire, versus a traditional phone call. In a video conference call, Starters can see nonverbal facial expressions.

A great example of how Starters operate is the way President Donald Trump ran his election campaign to become the president of the United States. He had never run for an elected political office before, but structured his campaign around rallies with large crowds in order to see people face to face.

He brought his Starter energy and charisma to the stage – and against all odds, won the election over a Finisher household name, Hillary Clinton – President Bill Clinton's first lady, who was a former U.S. senator, and a former secretary of state. She had been favored to win easily over Mr. Trump.

A conversation is filled with nonverbal cues and clues using body language. Starters instinctively know how important these cues are when presenting and communicating to connect with colleagues and clients. On the flip side, Finishers instinctively will try to do things in the most efficient way possible. Instead of driving or flying to see their clients, for the most part Finishers would rather send an email or text their people.

As a young Starter, John Goetz worked in a shoe factory. It was his first job and he was only there a short period of time – until he started to figure out that some people could love doing that kind of work for a large portion of their lives. He would question some of them: "So did you say that you have been here pulling tacks for 20 years, and this is all you have ever done?" They seemed to be excited to simply be there and have that type of work as their job. John would ask, "Tell me, how can you do this for so long?" As a Starter, he did not understand how they could see themselves doing that work for years.

John knew that particular job was not the most worthless thing in the world that he could do with his life. However, he felt negatively about the situation when he was in the middle of living that type of life. Today, in many parts of the world, there are machines that do that type of work. However, there are still very repetitive jobs that need to be done, and people still regularly fill those jobs.

We know that money is a powerful motivator. However, given the opportunity to choose, Starters are much more likely to choose jobs that involve quite a bit of human interaction and a variety of tasks or responsibilities. The process of successfully making customers and clients happy – to the point that they want to do business with the company for years to come – is very fulfilling to most Starters.

Finishers are more likely to stay with a company even when things seem tough and hard. It may not look like there is any success in sight. However, they are the ones that a company wants to hire and train because of their devotion to the organization and tendency to stay in the field longer. Starters love to bounce around where the new, fun energy is flowing – where there are signs and hopes of a bright future ahead that include new opportunities. Stability is not the greatest need they have in order to move through their lives successfully. Moreover, a Starter is more likely to leave his or her former life behind to make a fresh start.

Generally, Starters are the biggest risk-takers on the planet. This causes them to either be very successful or to land in bankruptcy court. They could be in trouble unless they are able to sell their ideas or gain investors to fund the project. If their idea does not succeed, Starters are able to say, "Oh well, it did not work out this time. Next time, we will be able to do much better because we have learned what did not work well."

Thomas Edison provides an example of this business strategy. It is said that people would come to him and ask him if he felt like a failure since so many things he tried did not work. He would reply with: "I have not failed. I've just found 10,000 ways that won't work."

All around the world, Starters are the ones who have much more faith and trust in their ability to connect with people emotionally, which gives them the best opportunity for future success. Personal relationships are huge for Starters when they are doing business with people. They tend to be more willing to go through ups and downs with people rather than to simply fire the person and move on to the next service provider.

Parents get extremely frustrated when they have helped their child go through college to get a degree, and then the child goes into a line of work that has little to do with that degree. Starter children are usually the ones that do this. They do not want to spend their life doing things that they do not want to do, no matter how much the job pays. Money is not the number one consideration for Starters when they are considering a career path. Meaning and purpose typically trumps being able to buy the latest new car or the biggest house on the block.

Because they open their hearts to the emotional needs of people, Starters make amazing caregivers. They have the ability to take people into their hearts to love and cherish for as long as they are able.

Starters tend to excel in a playfully productive environment. When companies make time for fun and ingenuity in the same space, Starters are more likely to be "all-in" and give their heart and soul to the company. Starters like to be a part of innovative projects that are emerging as something new in the marketplace.

Bill Gates is one of those people. I watched an interview where Mr. Gates said that when he read about the computer chip, he instinctively knew that this product was going to change the way the world works and interacts. He knew that the invention was going to be huge in the marketplace, and he wanted to be a part of the massive industry growth that would come because of the technology.

Mr. Gates had the vision, and was willing to start small when companies like IBM and others dismissed the microchip idea as trivial. As it turns out, Mr. Gates was correct – his company, which started very small, made him one of the richest people in the world.

There is often a good time for a Starter to take the conversation to the next step, connecting the benefits of a product to the consumer market. However, when discussing business, Starters enjoy the personal interaction so much that they will talk too long and in a circuitous manner, never getting the opportunity to execute the contract before losing the prospect's attention. Many times, the prospect will simply walk away, saying, "I'll have to get back to you." If a Starter is not careful and sensitive to the optimal timing involved in the sales process, they will lose sales. This is one of the reasons why it is good to send people out two by two. The Starter can be the one who sets the stage and prepares people's hearts to receive. Then, the Finisher can take care of the details, and fill a complementary role to teach and train.

That would be the ideal situation, although it is not always possible to organize teams that way. However, it is important to consider the increased success that this kind of teaming will bring to projects and objectives.

CHAPTER 9

Energy Within Gender

The book that really helped John understand that there was something more profound in human relations regarding the natures of men and women was a book about Samson and Delilah.

After reading, he closed the book and said, "This is not right. I am like Delilah and my wife is like Samson." Knowing that drove him to find answers. He would say, "What they are describing about men is not like me – and I am a man."

People on TV and radio talk shows would be preaching the same message, and John would say time and time again that the philosophy was not correct. What others were saying about a man's nature was not like him. He was not sure what to do about the fallacies, as he saw them, which were presented regularly as truth.

He determined that he was going to study to find out who God was. He would say that many people do not even understand who God is, and what His nature is like. He would also say, "Well, I know who God is now, and I do not have a problem with that at all. I clearly do not understand who mankind is, because applying what I hear being taught about men and women is just not working in my world for me."

So, he came to understand the difference in energy was not because people are men or women. It was not a female vs. male issue. It really was the energy level – the up-and-down energy or linear energy with which they were made that caused people to attract or repel others.

The PeopleLogics principles promote the concept that God created both men and women and that they are both vital for any large group of individuals to experience true success and happiness. Men and women can be in collaborative roles or supportive roles.

With that being said, let us now go into an overview of how the differences of men and women can be better understood and celebrated.

The Scriptures read that in the beginning, God created man with many amazing privileges and responsibilities – with the power to name the animals of the earth and personally commune with his Creator. If we could think of it from a business standpoint, things in the garden were thriving. The marvels of God's creations were being celebrated and there was much joy on earth.

There was still something missing. Adam did not have anyone to join with him to enjoy his successes on a deep, intimate level. He did not have another human at home to share a peaceful evening with, looking up at the vastness of the heavens, and celebrating the goodness of God.

God saw that this was not good, in part because He Himself is the master of relationships. He knew that since He loved Adam so much, having a companion for Adam that would complement him would bring much joy. That companion could hold his hand and share dreams about the times ahead when they would have the opportunity to experience new things and make memories that would last.

Adam's desires did get fulfilled, and his God did make an amazing companion for him to share the experience of life. I can only imagine how wonderful it must have felt to walk in perfect harmony, living their day-to-day life without the confines of arrogance and conceit. How wonderful it must have been when, everyday, they woke up and desired to experience something new that did not include pride and ego coming into the picture. There were no put-downs and condescending remarks. There was no cursing and slandering with tears at the end of their day due to one partner degrading their mate about their place in the world.

What a better place this world would be if we would just decide to do whatever it takes, take whatever course we need to take, as often as necessary, until we wake up each morning with the first thought, *What an amazing person God gave me with whom to experience life.*

Now it is time to begin to break down some of the misunderstandings that cause strife and division between men and women. One point is that while both men and women are created to be an awesome reflection of their Creator, they are not designed to be good at the same things or to be interested in pursuing the same agendas.

Men are not all alike, and women are not all alike. Starter women act and behave much differently than do Finisher women. While they both can give birth, they do not show up with the same desires and agendas.

There are many myths propagated and books written about how men are all one way and women are all another way. There are also many analyses about how to understand the opposite sex well. The fact is that, globally, approximately one-half of men are designed with the energy and traits of a Starter, while the other half of men are designed with the energy and traits of a Finisher. This also holds true for women.

Now is a great time for us to highlight the energy types of people of the same gender who are in similar industries. The following are some examples of differences among well-known people who are easily found on the internet – people who represent particular energy types.

The first example is the difference between Bill Murray, who starred in *Ghostbusters*, *What About Bob?*, and other hit comedies, and Daniel Craig, who played the secret agent James Bond in many films, such as *No Time to Die*.

Bill Murray is a Starter who is a free-spirited person. His free-flowing body movements and smile make it easy to quickly identify his energy type. His natural humor and wit makes him a very likable person to many. Daniel Craig, on the other hand, is a Finisher who is generally a very stoic individual with more deliberate body movements and facial expressions. Those traits are evident in his James Bond movies.

To help show that race has nothing to do with determining energy types, the following is an example of two actors of the same race with opposite energy types. Eddie Murphy is an American Starter actor and comedian who starred in movies like *Holy Man*, *A Thousand Words*,

The Nutty Professor, and *Dr. Dolittle*. His energy type makes him a witty comedian – a natural for being cast in jaw-dropping comedies. Samuel L. Jackson, on the other hand, is a Finisher American actor. He starred in movies like *The Man* and *Cleaner*. His intense attitude on film and in life make it easy for a person trained in PeopleLogics to determine that he is a Finisher.

Helen Hunt is an American Finisher actress and winner of numerous awards, including an Academy Award for Best Actress. John always liked her role in the hit movie *Twister*. She exemplifies a common trait of a Finisher at the end of the movie. The characters survived the storm, and instead of having a big celebration, Helen Hunt's character immediately starts to talk about working on what they learned from the experience.

Reese Witherspoon is a Starter who is also an actress and winner of numerous awards, including an Oscar for Best Actress. She has starred in movies like *Legally Blonde, Sweet Home Alabama,* and *This Means War.* She is a good example of an actress who has excelled by playing to her Starter strengths. Mostly, she brings fun and warm feelings to her starring roles in her movies.

Here are two first ladies of the United States who were members of the same political party during their time spent in the White House. First Lady Hillary

Clinton is the first woman in the history of the United States to win the nomination of the Democratic Party to run for president. And although Michelle Obama has many impressive accomplishments, she will always live in history as the first African American first lady to live in the White House.

Now we can highlight another way to gain insight into what energy types these two women possess. Focusing on the front covers of Hillary Rodham Clinton's books – *Her Way*, *A Woman in Charge*, and *Hard Choices* – we see that she is not smiling vivaciously in her pictures. She is a very direct, confident lady, and it shows in her photos. Moreover, her Finisher energy comes through in her narratives as she speaks in detail about facts and logical decision-making.

Michelle Obama's photos on the covers of her books *Becoming*, *In Her Words, Believe in the Possibility: The Words of Michelle Obama*, and *American Grown*, have captured her smiling with her beautiful bright teeth showing. Her fun, vibrant smiles popping off the covers attracts warm-hearted individuals to read her books. Michelle Obama is a Starter.

Next, we can go deeper into the political arena in the United States.

In the United States, the presidential nomination process usually starts with many candidates. When I was told that Donald Trump, who is a Starter businessman, was entering the race for the nomination of his party, I said, "I don't know if he is going to win, but he sure is going to make things interesting." During the campaign, Mr. Trump's Starter energy made it very easy for him to be witty and respond quickly without much thought about a topic.

He ended up serving as the 45th President of the United States. His charismatic energy and style captured the attention of millions of voters around the country who were mesmerized by his rallies and speeches. He was very good at ad-libbing during speeches, and gauged the audience's responses to guide his commentary. One of the ways he used his Starter energy was when he would include himself in with the crowd. For example, many times, he would say things like, "They are after us. They are trying to silence our voices."

Starters like Donald Trump are innately good at rallying support from a crowd based on emotions, versus using facts and figures. They do use facts and figures on a general basis; however, fact-checkers love to find mistakes in political Starters' statements, saying that the statements were not accurate, or not exact according to data. As we will be discussing in the next chapter, high-profile Starters like Donald Trump are naturals at connecting with large numbers of people, and good at causing them to be "all-in" to promote a cause that they feel is essential to improving the human condition.

Donald Trump and Michael Pence, the Finisher who served as Donald Trump's vice president, made a good team because they balanced each other's energy type. In the United States, the vice president is not elected, but chosen by the presidential candidate. An intriguing concept is that if one goes back through history in the United States, they will find that most of the time, the presidential candidate has chosen someone of the opposite energy type to run and serve alongside them.

Here are a couple of male Kings to compare, since they are such prominent figures in Christianity, Islam and Judaism.

King David was a Starter who was very spontaneous when it came to stepping up and killing his people's enemy, Goliath. David was a young shepherd who suddenly chose to take on a champion warrior. David won, and his fame spread throughout the land. As a classic Starter, David also wrote about extreme lows – like watering his couch with his tears, and feeling like his God had forsaken him. In David's writings and speech, he was emotional and talked to and about his God in a very personal way. Starters sometimes act with utter abandonment. An example of this in King David's life was when he came back to the city after winning a battle and danced before his God with all his might. His wife did not like it; but that will happen when people feel that Starters are acting irrationally.

On the other hand, King Solomon, King David's son, was a bit of a master of one-liners. His writing of most of the book of Proverbs is wisdom in bullet-point format. There is much to be gained and enjoyed in King Solomon's writing style, since, as a Finisher, he was apt to use fewer words to communicate major points of wisdom – unlike his father, King David.

In the United States, American football has a final game called the Super Bowl to determine the champion of the National Football League for the year. In the NFL, it is of utmost importance to have a good quarterback if the team expects to win the Super Bowl trophy.

Peyton Manning and Tom Brady are two of the all-time great quarterbacks. They both have won Super Bowls as starting quarterbacks, yet they have noticeably different energy.

Payton Manning is the one with the outgoing style that corporate advertisers love. In commercials with companies like Nationwide Insurance, he does most of the talking and comes across as very relaxed and quite humorous. Mr. Manning is the Starter of the two.

Tom Brady has won the most Super Bowls in the history of the NFL. As a Finisher, his commercials may not be the funniest, and he has been characterized as having a robotic persona. However, producing results on the field has been his trademark for years. As we discussed earlier, Finishers as a whole are better at responding well when pushed and under pressure.

An example of this is when Tom Brady and his team, the New England Patriots, broke the record for the largest comeback win in Super Bowl history in 2017. Toward the end of the game between the Patriots and the Atlanta Falcons, it seemed clear that the Falcons had won. The Falcons' owner walked down to the Falcons' side of the field with his wife with a smile on his face as he waved to the fans. The Falcons were ahead 28-3 with 8:31 left in the third quarter; the Falcons were up 25 points and it seemed like the rest of the game would just be a formality. Little did the Falcons' owner know that Tom Brady, as a Finisher, would be able to remain focused and not succumb to the pressure.

Mr. Brady and his team dialed up their game. The comeback was amazing; the score was tied at the end of the fourth quarter, and the game went into overtime. Eight plays later, Mr. Brady won the Super Bowl. If you want a closer, get a Finisher like Tom Brady to join your team.

CHAPTER 10

Diverse Energy Flows

You will find it extremely beneficial to develop your PeopleLogics skills to the point that you will be able to identify a person's energy type – even if they are across the room and you have not even spoken to them. Imagine the increased ability you will have at connecting with others, in virtually any situation, with these skills.

As stated earlier, there is too much conflict in the world due to the lack of understanding about what can encourage harmonious relationships versus conflicted ones. Knowing ahead of time that you are talking to someone with a different energy type, or a similar one, helps defuse conflict. That knowledge can bring enlightenment to the communication.

The following graphics are examples of the primary variations of how energy flows within the energy types.

Starter Energy

Medium-Profile Starter

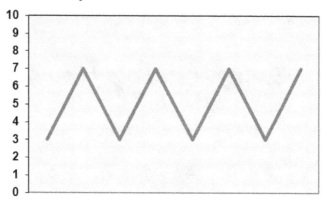

In Chapter 1, you were introduced to this type of energy and how it flows through people. The medium-profile Starter energy type is the most common within the Starter energy types. This energy is flowing through a person due to their DNA.

Low-Profile Starter

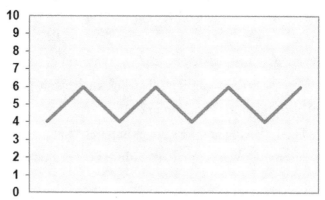

In the process of analyzing others and attempting to identify their energy types, and when it is not practical to ask the other person to do a PeopleLogics energy assessment, this energy type can be mistaken as a medium-profile Finisher (described later in this chapter). Since they have less energy swings, it makes it more difficult for someone to recognize them as being a Starter without additional training and experience, which is outside the scope of this book.

A low-profile Starter's energy still goes up and down rapidly, yet with less dramatic highs and lows. There was a time when I worked with an accountant who stayed very focused and had few dramatic shifts in behavior and energy. Since I had the opportunity to spend time with the accountant outside of the work environment, it became easy to identify the individual as being a Starter – even though she was quiet at times and communicated softly when speaking with others.

High-Profile Starter

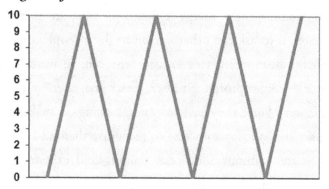

I am providing more content about this energy type, because the people with this type of energy are so much fun for me to write about.

A High-profile Starter's energy flows with dramatic shifts from extreme highs to extreme lows. This makes them some of the most outgoing, compassionate people on the planet. Since their energy shifts are so extreme, it is very important for them to be surrounded with people who they respect to "speak into their lives in love" – to help them direct their emotions and energy in positive, productive ways.

Just as high as they can get, is how low they can also go. This is why it is important to look at people who quickly go from laughing to crying, or from being full of passion and joy to yelling about something that might seem a bit trivial. Noticing these patterns will help you identify a high-profile Starter.

High-profile Starters can seem to many others as being a little flaky. However, they are usually very talented at encouraging and caring for others.

They can get excited over something very small, and it will make them feel as though they are on top of the world. The next moment, their energy can crash with one small comment from another, or because of an incident that others may think is not a big deal. This Starter energy type can become hypersensitive to comments that were said, or about a point that was brought up. They were feeling so good, but then you will see them hitting rock bottom. They will need some extra support to get back up to a normal energy flow. But it may only take a few moments before the next exciting thing comes along, and their energy level is back on top again.

Regarding this energy type, John would tell a story that went something like this: "I remember a businessman who came to our house one time, and said he was going to recruit enough people to go to the top of our company in six months. Later, I had trouble finding out whatever happened to him. Finally, I found out that he had gotten into a con game and ended up in jail. He was recruiting other people, but into the wrong kind of business." This is an example of how high-profile Starters can get so enthusiastic about something that they can get sucked into a con if they are not careful.

Finisher Energy

Medium-Profile Finisher

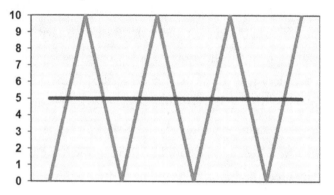

As presented in Chapter 1, John would draw out this medium-profile Finisher energy type when helping people understand who they were and how they were made. This is the most common type of energy that flows through Finishers on earth. It also is part of the basis of training others to understand the fundamentals of energy flow.

The medium-profile Finisher energy type has moderate energy fluctuations. They usually go through the day without major energy fluctuations or dramatic behavior shifts.

Low-Profile Finisher

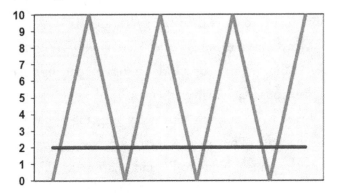

It is interesting how people desiring long-term partnerships are not only attracted to their complementary energy type, but also may find themselves more attracted to a higher or lower contrasting energy type – which takes the balance of nature to another level. For example, a low-profile Finisher is usually attracted to a higher-profile Starter.

One thing Finishers are very good at is keeping Starters from getting too high or too low. The Finisher's consistency provides security from the emotional roller coaster on which Starters frequently find themselves.

Low-profile Finishers can seem apathetic about topics and situations, while they actually deeply care about them. To get a Finisher's energy to move up, it usually takes longer and "louder" events with more stimuli; more energy to move their energy bar higher.

Many times, unenlightened Starters will say things like, "Come on, liven up a little," instead of putting them in situations that will liven them up."

I used to do business with a very outgoing gentleman and his wife. They owned their own business and he was very much high-profile and charismatic. She, in contrast, was very low-profile and quiet. She listened to his stories attentively, even though she had probably already heard them a hundred times over the years. They complemented each other well. They were a great example of a model couple.

On the other hand, it is said that too much of a good thing is too much of a good thing. Pairing a high-profile Starter and a high-profile Finisher usually is not a good idea – you will get a glimpse of that next.

High-Profile Finisher

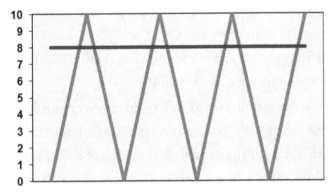

When trying to connect with another person, it is important to tune in to the other person's energy level and adjust your energy to match theirs to move them forward. If you are coming from a high place, and the person you are talking to has very low energy, you will simply blow them away instead of motivating them. It is a challenge for high-profile Finishers to interact with lower-energy people, since their energy stays so high and they can easily become overbearing and pushy.

The only time I ever heard my dad, John, express regret about inviting a person to visit at his parents' house was when he invited a high-profile Finisher over. He was so upset about how that Finisher came in and totally dominated the atmosphere there. John said that he would never do that again.

Still, if someone is needed to yell at players as they are competing in a sporting event, people with this energy type are a great choice. Or, if you need someone to defend your property or your nation, these people make outstanding leaders and warriors.

In the next chapter, we will continue by acknowledging that there are both functional and dysfunctional behaviors, which can occur in the different energy types. As we shine a light on them and learn about them, it is easier to help people change their behaviors from dysfunctional to functional.

CHAPTER 11

Functional and Dysfunctional Energy

There are many ways for us to find ourselves off course and living a dysfunctional life, versus a love-based life. In this chapter, we will discuss how, when we let our egos get in the way, we can become dysfunctional in some areas. We may find ourselves living in a way quite opposite to how our Creator intended.

The scriptures say: "Love your neighbor as yourself." When we step back and are honest with ourselves, most of us have to admit that there are too many times that we act to promote our own agenda. We act out of self-interest instead of considering what is in the best interest of others in the relationship. When we take a "win-win" stance in our relationship with others, our world becomes a more peaceful place to live. The problem is that there are too many people on the planet who do not want a "win-win," or a peaceful place to live. This is where dysfunction begins to form.

Dysfunction in Communication

Typically, Finishers think through what they are going to say – so much so that before they say it, they will remember, pretty much word for word, what they have said. They are more calculating with the words they use, or do not use, to communicate their message. When they are given time to think through what they are going to say, they will be able to communicate their ideas with great accuracy.

A Starter may say, "I thought you said you were going to the store and then to pick up Chinese takeout on your way home." But a Finisher may answer, "No, that is not what I said," because they are remembering their statement accurately.

Finishers can get extremely frustrated when they are misquoted by Starters. One of the reasons that Finishers are misquoted so often is because Starters will relate what they felt like the Finishers were really trying to say. The Starter did not focus on quoting the Finisher word for word. More times than not, they focused on the emotions behind the words that were said, and then repeated what they felt like the Finisher was really trying to say.

Starters tend to tune into the emotions and voice inflections. Starters will paraphrase a past conversation; they will interpret what the Finisher said, instead of verifying the exact wording and saying, "This is what I believe you said; is that correct?"

It frustrates the Finisher when they seem to get misquoted so often. Many times, the translation that Starters make about what was said, instead of listening to the actual words, causes statements to get altered.

And Finishers' statements may ignite some emotions in the Starters, who in turn may react in what seems to be an irrational way. Most of the time, when Starters are listening and talking, they are not communicating with logic in mind. They are coming back emotionally charged, especially if they are passionately communicating something that did not feel right about what the Finisher had to say.

When a Starter translates the conversation through their own internal filter and comes up with a conclusion, it causes great problems in relationships. While it is wise to understand that a Starter is instinctively going to continue to internally process communication this way, Finishers would be wise to prepare to clarify and repeat what they actually said – without entering into a hostile zone. Knowing that this kind of misinterpretation is going to happen regularly is a key to emotionally neutralizing this behavior's negative effect.

Finishers may say, "I know good and well what I said." That kind of response can quickly escalate the discussion into an argument, especially when there is not an acknowledgement by the Starter that they may not be quoting exactly what was said. The Starter may believe that it is enough to verbalize what they felt was actually meant by the other person.

It can come across as very cold and calculating to a Starter when Finishers say things that are clearly directed at the Starter's vulnerable emotions. Starters usually have a major issue with this happening to them time and time again, so they start to build invisible walls to protect their heart. Most of the time it would benefit Starters to say things like, "This is what it felt like, and came across to me like, when you spoke to me. What did you actually mean by what you said?"

When a Starter listens to a Finisher's words, the meaning of the words may feel different to the Starter in contrast to what was actually said. However, the words that the Finishers use are usually clear and are exactly what the Finisher meant to say.

Often, when Starters say something and then change their minds, Finishers may start to lose respect for them. But John Goetz addressed that topic this way: "It was my idea to start with. I should be able to change my mind about my own idea."

On the other hand, Starters are instinctively better at making light, fun remarks that defuse tension in a conversation so that people are more open to receive communication.

When operating in the dysfunctional mode, Finishers tend to make statements that are crafted in a way to sting and hurt Starters emotionally. One of the main reasons that Starters seem to respond irrationally at times is because they know in their heart that the verbal arrow that was just shot at them was calculated and premeditated.

Functional Communication

When Starters respond in order to find out what is really going on, they will probe the Finisher with more questions. The questions may be ones like, "Now, what were you saying exactly? What do you think about that now? I think I heard you say this; but what do you really think about what you said?" The Starter should just keep on probing – going deeper and deeper until getting to the real issue under the surface that is causing the disunity.

In that discussion, the Finisher may start off by saying something like, "Oh no, there is nothing going on here." The Starter will want to keep asking more questions, as long as they are ready to handle the arrows that are about to come flying at their heart and their emotions.

Starters should give Finishers a safe place in a less hostile environment so they can continue to verbalize their feelings and thoughts. Then the Starter will be able to get deep enough into the layers of grievances to find out what the main issue is behind the hostility. Then and only then will the two people be able to address the thing that has been lying there dormant, and festering for days, months, or even years.

When a Finisher talks about all the seemingly-trivial things that are causing hostility and frustration, many times Starters will get infuriated, because they will find it hard to believe that the Finisher had not moved on from that grievance a long time ago.

And most of the time, it is best for Finishers to resist the urge to come back and say, "But you said two hours ago. . ." Instead, they should just know up front that Starters talk to hear themselves think. A Finisher will not want to buy into a Starter's original statement unless it has been written out ahead of time or discussed multiple times.

In relationships involving married couples and partners, if the issues that the Finisher is hiding do not get brought out into the open, suddenly you will have weeks, months, and even years go by without a resolution. The relationship may just turn into one where the people involved are simply cohabitating and no longer enjoying full intimacy.

Not addressing personal attacks and hostile comments as they come up will only lead to more resentment and distance as Starters start to build up walls to protect their hearts. The Finishers will become more and more distant in the relationship.

At the beginning of a relationship, the Starter may want to say to the Finisher, "In this relationship, no matter what you have experienced before, we are going to do everything possible to live in harmony with each other. In this relationship, we are going to focus on communicating about the issues within a reasonable time frame from when they happen. In this relationship, if you expect to stay with me, we must have an open dialogue. We are not going to allow a list of 10 or 20 items that you have against me to build up before we ever talk about the first one."

"I am going to make this as safe a place as possible so that when you bring up these things, I will not purposefully attack you. But we are going to deal with the issues, because I know that God made you a Finisher and me a Starter, and we each bring complementary attributes and extreme value to the table. As a Starter with up-and-down energy, I am not going to finish and follow through with everything I initiate. To help us understand each other better and who each of us really are, we must agree that we are going to discuss these things along the way."

Moving from Dysfunctional to Functional

Both Starters and Finishers can get into such a dysfunctional mode that they can go "off the charts." It is important to identify when this has happened. It is possible to get addicted to "the highs" – and when this happens, it may become necessary to talk to someone that can bring clarity and practicality to the situation.

For instance, when the leaders of companies have grandiose, impractical ideas, they have CFOs – chief financial officers – to bring them back down to reality. The CFO can let the other corporate leaders know that they do not have the money to carry out certain ideas. Having a practical voice on the team helps the leadership pursue a more realistic agenda. The company can make plans that they can financially afford to do at that time.

The same dysfunctional behavior can be found in everyday life regarding finances. Starters, for instance, can be impulsive when it comes to spending, which causes them to get in financial trouble. Just the other day, my friend called me from West Palm Beach. He said that he was stuck and that he could not afford a $189 tire to put on his vehicle. As it turned out, he was driving a virtually new Jaguar SUV, but his credit was so bad that he could not put even $200 on a credit card to pay for the tire.

It may require getting a financial mentor to help someone move from a dysfunctional style in managing personal finances to a functional, healthy style that includes emergency reserves and a savings account.

Those in a dysfunctional relationship need to understand the necessity of not dominating the relationship – but spending time with, and paying attention to, someone other than themselves. Conversations will necessitate listening as well as talking – and taking care to understand what is said, while not interrupting the other person.

A major dysfunction in personal partnerships is a desire to change one's partner. Many times as the relationship develops, one of the partners moves from the position of mutual respect to trying to change the other person. As a result, one person could begin speaking to their partner like a parent would speak to a child.

As John would say, "Who wants to sleep with and have sex with their parent?" When one partner develops a superior attitude in the relationship, real intimacy dwindles. A functional, healthy personal partnership requires a belief that the other person is not broken and does not need fixing by you.

Finishers are more focused and get to the point more quickly than do Starters. This can be a positive trait to possess. However, it can become dysfunctional when a Finisher jumps to a conclusion of what needs to happen without first talking about the thought process that they went through to get to that conclusion. And Finishers can become angry and annoyed about having to endure verbal hostility from others about something that they have already reasoned out as the best plan of action. Finishers will want to become aware that they need to focus on going completely back to the beginning of the thought process with others, and lead them to the plan and solution.

Starters are very good at responding quickly to new opportunities and leaving their past behind to start a new job or business venture. When this becomes dysfunctional is when Starters get addicted to the high and exhilaration of starting new ventures. They do not sit down and assess the costs that their decisions will have on their lives and the people around them. As we discussed before, bankruptcy courts are full of Starters who have entered into the dysfunctional realm, and acted on their feelings instead of sound financial advice. Jumping from idea to idea has a cost. The functional Starter, when faced with a new, exciting opportunity, will want to carefully consider the full financial risk and emotional impact – not only on themselves, but also on the spouse and children, as they may move to a new location and lose friendships. A wise Starter will seek counsel from someone who is less emotionally involved in the outcome of the situation.

Living a Functional Life

A wise person is one who shows love and understanding while practicing good judgment when interacting with others. Living a functional life all comes down to wanting to operate in unconditional love when interacting with others; loving others at least as much as we love ourselves.

CHAPTER 12

A Lesson in Love

John Goetz never liked to close without presenting the message of love versus fear. The following are his exact words:

*When a person is born, they are born in love. A loving little baby has not yet learned to fear. From birth, one can move in one of three primary directions – toward **superiority fear**, **inferiority fear**, or toward **unconditional love**. The progression usually starts in early childhood when their parents speak words over their children. At the beginning of life, parents are usually the primary factor in determining the direction a child moves. Parents instill beliefs in their children from the time they are born.*

*If the parents degrade their child with wounding words such as "you are no good" or "you will never amount to anything" or "you are a stupid little brat," the child may learn to feel **inferior**. Next, when the child goes to school,*

147

similar things may happen there that perpetuate the feeling of inferiority. If the child's peers begin to put the child down for not wearing designer clothes, or for being overweight, the child develops a deep-rooted sense of inferiority. The child begins to believe they are too short, or too dumb, or deficient in some way. They hear "no" so much that they start to feel like something is wrong with them. So, they start putting themselves down. Later, the child becomes even more sensitive to the things around them that reinforce their belief system that they are inferior. For example, the child may be really poor in sports, or they may ask a question in class that makes others think they are not very smart. Later in life, maybe all they can afford is to live on the wrong side of town or shop at the second-hand store, or ask for charity from time to time. Maybe they are obese, lack a college degree, work at a menial job, or are single or divorced, etc.

Were words spoken over you that affected you to move toward inferiority?

If the parents teach their child attitudes such as "you are so much better than those trashy people" or "we don't hang around with those kinds of people, they live on the wrong side of town," the child may learn to feel **superior**. The superiority belief system **may** start subtly, but still progresses over time to have a major effect on a person's belief system. The parents may give the child too much *technology, too many toys, or the best clothes, etc. Maybe the child lives in the nicest part of town. The child may begin to feel better than others because they are more attractive or have better things, and develop an inflated self-esteem, a high ego, an "I'm better than you" attitude. Later, as an adult, the person may feel superior because they have so many good things in life, such as a fancy luxury car, athletic skills, the latest cell phone, a prestigious degree, or a corner office with a view. They feel superior because of so many material possessions.*

No matter whether a child develops an attitude of inferiority or one of superiority, both are still operating in fear. Though the sides of this fear may seem opposite, they are in the same pit of fear. Instead of moving up toward unconditional love, they are moving down into fear. Fear also can be a negative addiction. People can become addicted to this negative lifestyle.

*The best way to raise a child is with **unconditional love**. You love and encourage and nurture them without talking down to them or teaching them to talk down to or about other people. You teach them that they have worth and value. You train them with affection and discipline. You teach them to stay in the middle of love, where they are not feeling inferior or superior, but are moving toward unconditional love in everything they do. Ideally, a parent* can give a child a huge advantage by using the example of Mary and Jesus' relationship as how one should raise a child. Mary taught Jesus from birth who He was and what He could become. Mary knew what she had; what a gift her baby was. She taught Him and trained Him in the ways of love from the beginning. People came and honored Him, as did she. She believed in Him. She even encouraged Him to perform His first miracle, after teaching Him and training Him to live a love-based lifestyle. As He became an adult and started His ministry, the common people heard Him gladly. He was also encouraged by His own heavenly Father who said, **"This is my beloved son, in whom I am well pleased."** This is an example of the kinds of words parents should speak over their children to help them develop a healthy self-esteem and a healthy ego. Jesus lived His life in service to mankind and fulfilled the words, "No greater love has this that a man should lay down his life for his friends." Thus we are offered the ultimate example of what true unconditional love is all about. HE is the one person we know for sure who was born in love and remained in love continually throughout His life all the way to the cross.

Based on environmental influences, people have an opportunity to move toward fear or toward unconditional love.

This can happen at any stage of life. A decision at any moment in life can be made that I am going to start moving toward love, no matter how I was raised. How can you reverse the curse? For those living with inferiority fear, one way you can do this is to encourage yourself. Look at yourself in the mirror and say, "I like myself." Use positive affirmations to build up your self-esteem. For those of you who are operating in inferiority fear, do not speak against wealth. It is not wise to speak against what you need to help you get out of your situation. Examples are Solomon's words when he says, "Laziness lets the roof leak and soon the rafters begin to rot." Ecclesiastes 10:19-20 reads, "A feast is made for laughter, and wine maketh merry: but money answereth all things. Curse not the king, no not in thy thought; and curse not the rich in thy bedchamber. . ."

For those living in superiority fear, one way is to become a giver and grow in compassion. You can visit children's hospitals, give anonymously to charity, volunteer at a school or an orphanage – do things that do not feed your ego.

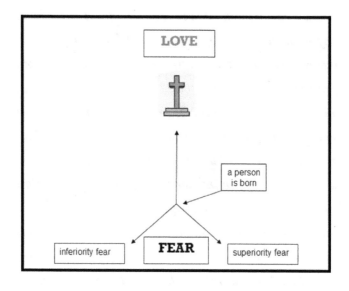

Conclusion

In this book, you have been introduced to some powerful principles about how to improve human relations and live a more harmonious life by understanding how you, and the people with whom you interact, were made. The principles of PeopleLogics work. You will want to learn them and use them to produce harmony with others, even though it may seem foreign to their way of thinking.

To continue your journey to the next level, you will want to go to *www.PeopleLogics.com*, where you will find additional information on other resources, and how to become a certified PeopleLogics trainer yourself.

As a trainer, you will get to know us and other individuals at a deeper level, which will provide you with the opportunity to help the most people and improve your understanding as well. Once I was told that one of the best ways to retain information was to listen to the content as if I were going to teach it to someone else. That is exactly what we are helping you to do when you enroll in our training program. As a certified trainer, you will be able to speak with confidence with others about what you have learned. You will then bring more value to others, and help them become more empowered to use the principles to improve their life.

Favor can open many doors. When people know and see that you understand them more completely than others do, they will want to know more. You are the answer to someone else's problem. You can bring hope where there is despair, and transform the lives of those you touch.

John wanted this message to be taught to people around the world. To do that, we desire your help. Please share and refer this book to as many people as possible, and lead them to *www.PeopleLogics.com*, where they will find resources and information on how to enroll in training classes. Thank you so much for taking these steps to begin your new journey.

Acknowledgments

What an amazing journey this has been. It is the culmination of some of my experiences and stories about how I was mentored and trained by my father, John Goetz. I have never been able to run far from my assignment to help him get his message out.

At this time, I would like to thank my wife Laura, who kept reminding me that this project was not something I could delegate to someone else. She continued to remind me that God told me to help Him get his message out. As it turns out, one of the best ways to do that is to write a book that people around the world can read and study.

Next, I would like to thank my publisher, April O'Leary. It was very clear that she was the one to work with to publish this book. Her amazing balanced spirit was confirmation to me that I made a good decision to follow my inner prompting to reach out to her. She was the first person I had ever spoken with to be my publisher. Once again I am amazed how well God knows how to pick the good ones that He wants to help fulfill His will on the earth.

Next, I would like to thank Kat, my Finisher editor. As we were finishing this project, she said, "Well, I guess it does take a Finisher." I knew what she meant. Thanks, Kat, for your work on this project.

As you may have discovered, I love to train others to help them grow in the areas in which I know something about. When I was a little stalled, towards the end of this project, I was enjoying training my wife's grandbaby how to pick out songs on my smartphone. As it turned out, he chose "Unwritten" by Natasha Bedingfield. This was significant because he was only about 6 months old at the time. It was a fun inspiration, and a great song to listen to. It reminded me once again that I was the only one who could speak the words on my lips. The rest is still unwritten.

Finally, I would like to thank my mother for all of her support and training throughout the years. Her love and kindness is cherished and has grown as the years have gone by. She will be in my heart forever. Thanks for everything you have ever done to show me love.

About The Author

Nathaniel John Goetz is an American author and human relations trainer, who believes that no nation or group of people has a monopoly on good ideas. He has a degree in sales and marketing management, which he has used as a foundation to develop his skills in many industries while he learned and improved his human relations expertise. Most significantly, through the teachings of John Goetz, his father and mentor, he learned that there is an easy way to understand people, and why they act and react the way they do – even if one does not know them well. In many cases, an individual may have never spoken to the other person; yet, they will be able to have incredible insight into why they behave the way they do and how to navigate relationships in a mutually-beneficial way. Now, he is committed to sharing the insights that were imparted to him to as many people as possible, so they can live a more harmonious life with whom they interact.